Jesus Calls

Justo L. González

ABINGDON PRESS
Nashville

JESUS CALLS

By Justo L. González

This book is printed on acid-free, elemental chlorine-free paper.

Scripture quotations, unless otherwise indicated, are from the New Revised Standard Version of the Bible, copyright © 1989, by the Division of Christian Education of the National Council of the Churches of Christ in the United States of America, and are used by permission. All rights reserved.

ISBN 0687-00740-2

05 06 07 08 09 10 11 12 13 — 10 9 8 7 6 5 4 3 2

MANUFACTURED IN THE UNITED STATES OF AMERICA

Contents

Meet the Writer 4
A Word of Welcome 5
How to Use This Resource 6
1. Jesus Calls Into Existence 7
2. Jesus Calls Into Discipleship 19
3. Jesus Calls by Naming and Renaming 31
4. Jesus Calls Into Death and Life 43
5. Jesus Calls Into Family 55
6. Jesus Calls Into Service 69
7. Jesus Calls Through Others 81
8. Jesus Calls Into Mission 91

Meet the Writer

Justo L. González, a United Methodist minister born in Cuba, is a retired member of the Río Grande Conference of the United Methodist Church. After his basic college and seminary education in Cuba, he came to study at Yale University, where he obtained three degrees: S.T.M. (1958), M.A. (1960), and Ph.D. (1961). In 1961, he joined the faculty of the Evangelical Seminary of Puerto Rico, teaching historical theology; and in 1969, he moved to Atlanta, where he now resides, in order to teach at Candler School of Theology (Emory University). Since 1977, he has been engaged in two main occupations: writing and promoting the theological education of Latinas and Latinos.

Along the line of the first of these interests, he has published over 80 books as well as hundreds of articles, both at the academic and at the popular level. Several of his books are used as textbooks in seminaries and colleges and are translated into Portuguese, Korean, Chinese, German, Japanese, and Russian. His interest in promoting the theological education of Latinas and Latinos led to the founding of the Asociación para la Educación Teológica Hispaña and of the Hispanic Summer Program, a program in theological education sponsored by 38 seminaries and universities. He was also the first executive director of the Hispanic Theological Initiative, a program based at Princeton Theological Seminary and funded by The Pew Charitable Trusts whose purpose is to support Latinos and Latinas pursuing advanced degrees in theology. Both of these interests are combined in many of his publications, including the journal *Apuntes*, which he edited for 20 years, and the publication of a 14-volume Spanish translation of the works of Wesley, which he also edited.

A Word of Welcome

Welcome to JESUS CALLS, an eight-session study of several biblical accounts of how Jesus calls people and what these accounts suggest for contemporary Christian life. Through an exploration of various aspects of the call of Jesus, you will

- understand that the call of Jesus not only invites and summons, it also creates, recreates, shapes, and empowers;
- see that the call of Jesus is not always a dramatic call to something unusual or heroic, but that it can also come as a series of calls experienced as minor steps in daily life;
- explore the way our discipleship takes shape according to our view of Jesus;
- explore the cross of Jesus and the relationship of suffering and self-denial in the call that invites us to discover our true selves;
- explore how the church is a family, how this relates to our own calling from Jesus, and how it may help in responding to difficulties now facing the family as an institution;
- understand that Jesus calls us and meets us through serving others;
- see that the call of Jesus can come through other people, both inside and outside the church;
- understand the Great Commission as both a calling and a sending into witness and service.

This study offers many opportunities to rediscover God's continuing call to discipleship through Jesus and the ways this call can revitalize faith and commitment to Jesus Christ in the contemporary world. We invite you to look closely at ways Jesus calls you to fulfill God's potential in your life. We pray that you will be richly blessed as you find meaning and new life in response to the call of Jesus Christ.

How to Use This Resource

We hope you enjoy participating in this study, either on your own or with a group. We offer these hints and suggestions to make your study a success.

JESUS CALLS is a self-contained study with all the teaching/learning suggestions conveniently located on or near the main text to which they refer. They are identified with the same heading (or close abbreviation) as the heading in the main text. In addition to your Bible, all you need to have a successful group or individual study session is provided for you in this book.

Some special features are provided as well, such as the **Bible 301** activities in the teaching helps. We usually think of the "101" designation as the beginning level; these "301" designations prompt you to dig deeper. In these instances you will be invited to look up Scriptures, key words, or concepts in a Bible dictionary, commentary, or atlas. On occasion, an added book or resource is cited that may be obtained from your local library or perhaps from your pastor. Those resources are extras; your study will be enriched by these added sources of information, but it is not dependent on them.

This study is intentionally invitational. In the closing activity, you are invited to do three things: (1) to give prayerful consideration to your relationship to Jesus Christ and to make or renew your commitment, (2) to offer your own spoken prayers, and (3) to pray with and for others. We trust you will participate in these activities as you feel comfortable and that you will use them as a challenge to deepen your relationship with Jesus Christ.

Session One

Jesus Calls Into Existence

Session Focus ■
This session focuses on the importance of calling and naming. What makes the call of Jesus authoritative is not just that his teachings are good, or that he is a wise teacher. Jesus' call is authoritative beyond any other, because it is the continuation and the fulfillment of the initial call that has brought us into existence.

Session Objective ■
To place the entire study of the call of Jesus within its wider context. In the case of this call, calling is not just inviting or summoning; it is also creating and re-creating, shaping and empowering. Heeding the call of Jesus empowers us to follow him. His call both invites and provides the means to respond to that invitation.

Session Preparation ■
Compare the beginning of the gospels of Mark, Matthew, Luke, and John. Compare the beginning of John with the beginning of Genesis.

(John 1:1-14)

The Story Begins

When telling a story, one must first decide where to begin. In this regard, each of the evangelists made a different decision. Mark, who most scholars agree wrote before the other evangelists, declares in his very first words that he is starting at the beginning: "The beginning of the good news of Jesus Christ, the Son of God" (Mark 1:1). He then goes on to tell us about John the Baptist preparing the way for Jesus. Apparently Matthew did not think that this was starting early enough. It was necessary to show how Jesus connected with the entire history of Israel. Thus, he opens his Gospel: "An account of the genealogy of Jesus the Messiah, the son of David, the son of Abraham" (Matthew 1:1). Beginning with Abraham, he lists 56 generations connecting Abraham with Jesus. But even that was not enough for Luke. He begins his story with the births of John the Baptist and of Jesus; but then he connects this back to the beginning with a genealogy that, unlike Matthew's, goes all the way back to Adam (Luke 3:23-38).

Now John goes even further. It is not enough to begin the story of Jesus with the calling of John the Baptist. It is not enough

The Story Begins ■

If someone were to ask you to tell your story, where would you begin? Would you begin with your birthplace? with your parents? with your education? with the beginning of your career? with your conversion?

What would you say if someone were to say that your story begins "before the foundation of the world" (see Ephesians 1:4)?

Briefly tell your own stories to one another, beginning at different points: birth, joining the church, and finally "before the foundation of the world." How do these stories sound different? How do the starting points give each narrative a different flavor?

A Word Is More ■ Than a Sound

Can you remember a time or an occasion when you were "down" or "blue," and someone's word of encouragement helped you? Can you remember cases when the opposite was true—when someone's negative word seemed to have destructive power over you? Look around you and decide that today you will pronounce at least one "blessing"—one "good word"—over someone.

to begin with Abraham. It is not even enough to begin with Adam. One must go back to the very beginning, even before creation: "In the beginning was the Word, and the Word was with God, and the Word was God" (John 1:1). By the very wording of this opening statement, and by relating it to the creation of all things in verse 2, John is clearly relating this beginning to which he refers with the beginning of Genesis: "In the beginning God made . . . ." He will connect the events in the life of Jesus with the very beginning of Creation by declaring that Jesus is that Word who was in the beginning, and through whom all things were made, now made flesh, and having lived among us, so that we have been able to see his glory (John 1:14).

A Word Is More Than a Sound

There is a common saying that we often teach children in the hope that they will not react too violently to name-calling by their peers: "Sticks and stones may break my bones, but words will never harm me." While this may have prevented many a playground fight, it simply is not true. Words have the power to harm and to heal. Even in the case of the very children who are taught not to pay too much attention to name-calling, we do know that verbal abuse can be just as destructive as physical abuse. We know that a child who is repeatedly told that he is bad will very likely become a bad child, and one who is told that she is loved will have a better chance of growing up to be a loving person. Many of us, if asked about those experiences in which someone has hurt us most deeply, will refer to something someone said, rather than to something they did. And likewise, when asked who has helped us heal from our

Consider your own name. Do you know what it means? Were you named after somebody in your family? What expectations does your name place on you? Do you feel those expectations as a boon or as a burden? If you had a chance to rename yourself, what name would you take? Why? (You may wish to bring to the session a book explaining the meaning of various names. There is also a Web site where you can find the meaning of most names: *www.behindthename.com*.)

deepest wounds, many of us will remember something someone said just as much as something they did. Words are more than sounds. They have power.

That is one of the reasons why we put so much thought into the names we give our children. Obviously, sometimes children are given a name simply as a way to honor someone in the family, or perhaps a religious, national, or cultural hero. But even in those cases, when we give a child such a name, we are expressing the hope that this child will grow up to be like that family member or that hero. I was given my father's and my grandfather's name, hopefully as a way to honor them. This name (*Justo*) means "righteous," or "just." My classmates used to tease me claiming that I contradicted Scripture, which says that "There is no one who is righteous [in Spanish, "justo"], not even one" (Romans 3:10). Many years ago, a colleague told me that she had noticed how often that word appeared in Scripture readings when I planned a service. She may have been right: I may have been subconsciously selecting readings that included that word. But after she said this, and I began to notice that word, I found it almost inescapable in Scripture. It appears just about everywhere! In any case, as I look back on my early years, it was sometimes a challenge for me to be what my name said, and sometimes a burden, knowing that I was far from what my name claimed; but it was always present and powerful.

The power of words is also seen in the original meaning of *blessing* and *cursing*. Both in Latin and in Greek—as well as in several modern languages—"to bless" is to speak well of, and "to curse" is to speak evil of. We still have a remnant of that idea in English when we refer to a blessing as a "benediction" (*bene-dictio*, a "good saying") and to a curse as a "malediction" (a "bad or evil saying"). A blessing or benediction is powerful because it pronounces a good word over someone. Since what God speaks becomes a reality, God's good word on us becomes a good reality— a blessing. Likewise, a malediction or curse is thought to have the power of the evil word spoken over someone.

The Power of the Word of God

If this is true of mere human words, it is much more so in the case of the Word of God. John says that the Word of God is so far-reaching that it encompasses everybody and everything. In order to make the point absolutely clear, he states it first in positive terms, and then negatively. *All* things were made through the Word. Without the Word, *nothing* was made. There is not one atom, one distant star, one bird or beast that does not owe its very existence to the Word of God. In consequence, the entire history that follows about the incarnation of the Word and the life and teachings of Jesus has to do, not just with believers but with all of creation. That is what John is saying.

In a way, these first words of John are simply restating what the very first chapters of the Bible say. If John opens his book with the same words as in Genesis, "In the beginning," doing so is because he is relating the very beginning of all things to the message and the call of Jesus. Back in Genesis, God is depicted as making all things by speaking them. "Then God said, 'Let there be light'; and there was light." After that first creative pronouncement, God keeps on speaking; and what God utters leaps into existence. "Let there be . . . and there was."

This is why all good things that come

The Power of the Word of God ■

Close your eyes. Imagine a time before all time, a place beyond every place— the beginning. Now imagine God calling your name: "Let there be _____." See yourself leaping into existence at this majestic call. Pray that you may be true to this primal calling, to the very purpose of your creation.

from God are called "blessings" (remember: *blessing = bene-dictio = good word or saying*): they are the result of a good word from God—a word that brings them into existence. All of creation is good, because it has been made by a good word from God.

Thus, the Word of God is none other than the creative power of God. As John clearly states, the Word is not only "with God," but actually "is" God. The Word is God speaking, God creating. This is why the psalmist says that when the people were sick, oppressed, and in darkness, God "sent out his word and healed them, / and delivered them from destruction" (Psalm 107:20). This is why in Isaiah 55:11 God says: "So shall my word be that goes out from my mouth; / it shall not return to me empty, / but it shall accomplish that which I purpose, / and succeed in the thing for which I sent it." This does not mean simply that the Word of God will make itself heard, so that people will do what it says. It means also and above all that the Word itself acts in order to bring about God's will. Note that the text literally says that the Word of God "will accomplish" God's purpose, and will "succeed."

Along these lines, it may help to remember that we attribute a similar power to human words. When human pronouncements are not backed up by reality, we say that they are "empty words." Words (even human words) that are not "empty" have power. Speaking in such terms, it is important to assert and remember that the Word of God is never empty.

Jesus, the Word of God

Jesus, the Word of God ■

What do the words "*the Word became flesh*" suggest

What John ultimately says is that this Word who was in the beginning with God, this Word through whom all things are to you? What implications do these words hold for you in living out your daily life?

made, this Word that is none other than God is the One whom we have seen in Jesus Christ, for "the Word became flesh and lived among us, and we have seen his glory, the glory as of a father's only son, full of grace and truth" (verse 14). In some ways, this fourteenth verse of John's first chapter is the very core of the Gospel.

Late in the fourth century, Saint Augustine commented that he had found in the writings of the philosophers almost everything that John says in these first 14 verses. The one thing he did not find in them was this astonishing affirmation that the Word became flesh. The ancients knew of the power of words. They knew that words are intimately related to thought and reason. They also knew that what makes a human word powerful is its truth and its rationality. Therefore, they often spoke of the very principle that makes the world understandable, of its ultimately rational structure, as the "word" or *logos*—from which we derive the English word *logic*. The word *logos* implies that reality has an order that is similar to the order of our minds and of our words. If we can understand the world at all, it is because it shares in the rational structure of which words also partake. All of this Augustine found in the ancient philosophers whom he read.

John agrees that words are powerful, and in particular, that the Word of God is the divine creative power itself. But he adds that this Word, this creative power, this reason behind all things became flesh in Jesus Christ. This Augustine did not find in the writings of the ancient philosophers, even though they wrote so persuasively about the Word of God. This is the uniqueness of the Christian gospel.

What all this means is that Jesus is the Word of God. Not merely that Jesus speaks in the name of God, or teaches what God wishes to have taught, but that Jesus is the Word of God that was in the beginning— the Word through whom all things were made. He is the Word that said, "Let there be . . . ", and there was!

Jesus Calls Into Existence

This is crucial for our study, "Jesus Calls." Our very first call from Jesus did not come the first time we heard his name, or the first time we decided to follow him. Our first call from Jesus is none other than our call into existence. Before I could respond; before I knew it; even before I existed, the Word of God said, "Let there be Justo." That is why I am, and without that, I would not be! And the same Word has also said, "Let there be Mary"; "Let there be Juan"; "Let there be Richard"; "Let there be Jong-Hoon."

Whether we believe in him or not; whether we obey him or not; whether we follow him or not, we *are* because the Word of God has called us into existence.

In the sessions that follow, we shall be studying different aspects of the call of Jesus. Some will sound joyful and promising; others will seem harsh and demanding; but each and every one of them is based on his prior claim to our very existence precisely because Jesus is the Word made flesh, the Word through whom all things were made. This is why the words of John are so disturbing: "The world came into being through him; yet the world did not know him. He came to what was his own, and his own people did not accept him" (verses 10-11). He did not come as an interloper into a world and into human lives alien to him. He does not call us to an alternative among many. He calls us as his own. His call has authority because, will it or not, we are his own.

There is more. If the Word of God is God's creative power, this means that the call of Jesus, the call from the Word, is not just an invitation to try to do something. Too often we think that the call of Jesus is like a challenge to do our best, to try harder, to achieve something. It certainly is good to do our best, to try harder, and to achieve something. Even so, this is not all that the call is about. The call is also an act of new creation. When Jesus calls someone away from his nets, or his tax-collector's bench, or her occupation, that call has the same power as the one who said, "Let there be . . . ." That call not only invites the person to a new life but also creates that new life—or at least provides the power so that it may be so, if we but heed the call.

It is important for us to remember this central belief as we move along in our study, for otherwise the call of Jesus may appear to be an impossible burden. Indeed, we shall be called to undertake or at least to consider some difficult things—things so difficult, that quite frankly they are well beyond our power. Jesus will even speak of taking up the cross, and of giving up one's life—things that none of us would normally want to do, much less be able to do. If we take all of this as a mere challenge, much as a football coach challenges a team to greater effort, we shall necessarily fail. On those terms, probably we shouldn't even consider the call of Jesus, for we are certain to fall short of the mark.

The call of Jesus is more than an invitation. The call of Jesus is also his very act of calling us with the same power that called us from nothingness into existence. What the

Word of God names, the Word of God does. In consequence, the call of Jesus—whatever shape it might take, as we shall see in the sessions that follow—is not just an invitation but also a promise and a redefinition. It not only asks us to become followers; it makes us followers. It not only offers new life; it produces and gives new life.

Calling and Naming

Calling and Naming ■

In English, as in most Western languages, when we "call" someone, we may be doing one of two things: either summoning or naming. Calling is summoning, as when I say, "Winston, please come here." And calling is also naming, as when his parents decide to call a child Winston. In both cases, Winston is called. However, my calling him is a summons, while his parents' calling him is a naming. There is an obvious connection between the two, for once a person is named, that name is the most common way of summoning. When a child is born, after much debate, her parents decide to call her Stephanie. They may have debated for some time whether she would be Stephanie, Susan, or Louise. But once they have named her, whenever they wish to summon her, they call for "Stephanie." A name is a convenient way to call someone, or to identify that person. That is why in "CB" parlance, people refer to a *name* as a "handle." But the two meanings of calling are also connected; because when Winston's parents named him Winston, or Stephanie's parents named her Stephanie, they were also summoning them to live up to whatever Winston or Stephanie they were named after.

When Jesus calls us, he not only summons us, he also gives us, so to speak, a new name, a new identity, a new "handle," a new reality.

Can you imagine what would happen if we all had the same last name, "Godschild"? What would happen in a church where everyone was named, not after his or her earthly parents but after the heavenly one? What would be lost? What would be gained? (Why do you think that in the tradition of baptism the last name of the person is not used? One says, for instance, "I baptize you, Mary . . ."; and not "I baptize you, Mary Smith . . ." How might this be seen as a sign that the person's family name is now "Christian"–or, as suggested above, "Godschild"? What does this practice suggest about living one's life as a member of God's family?

Using a different imagery, the Gospel of John refers to this idea as being "born anew." Later on, we shall consider the specific case of Simon, whom Jesus renamed "Peter." But such renaming or rebirth is true of everyone whom Jesus calls—even if we do not literally change our name as a result.

This is why in the Book of Revelation there are so many references to "names," and in particular to new names. For instance: "To everyone who conquers . . . I will give a white stone, and on the white stone is written a new name that no one knows except the one who receives it" (Revelation 2:17). "If you conquer. . . , I will not blot your name out of the book of life; I will confess your name before my Father and before his angels" (Revelation 3:5). A name is a person's very identity. A hidden name is what a person is to be, but is not yet manifested. (Compare with Colossians 3:3).

Now go back to the text from John we are studying and look again at verse 12, where we are told that, although Jesus came to his own and his own did not receive them, those who did receive him and believe in him have been given "power to become children of God." Remember that in that setting it was customary to distinguish various people with the same first name by referring to their father's name. Thus, the name of Simon, who will later be called Peter, is "Simon son of Jonah" (Matthew 16:17) or, according to another tradition, "Simon son of John" (John 21:15). And James son of Zebedee is distinguished from James son of Alphaeus (for instance, in Mark 3:17-18). This custom, quite prevalent among many different peoples and traditions, is the origin of many last names even to this day. This is true not only in obvious cases such as Johnson and

Davidson but also of other names such as McDavid (son of David), Petersen (son of Peter), and even my own González (son of Gonzalo). On this basis, to become "children of God" is to take on a new name. Simon bar Jonah—the son of Jonah—is now Simon "Godschild." And so are Mary and Martha, and Paul and Barnabas, and you and I! No matter what our physical ancestry, no matter what our nationality, culture, or race, we bear the same last name. All who have believed in the Word Incarnate are one family, all with a common last name, "children of God."

This sounds like an extraordinary and exceptional thing. In many ways it is. Many of the first readers of John, upon hearing that they were children of God, would have contrasted that status in the eyes of God with their status in the eyes of the world—for many of them were poor, ignorant, despised by the world. Even today, believing in Jesus and heeding his call, and thus becoming a child of God, often marks a contrast between those who believe and the rest of humankind. There are still societies where Christians are excluded from public life, fired from their jobs, or rejected by their families. Thus, both because it proclaims a status that the world does not acknowledge and because it often sets believers apart, there seems to be a radical discontinuity between the common life of the rest of humankind and the life of those who believe.

On the other hand, that is only one side of the coin. The other is at least as important, and probably more: Those who believe are being called not to some newly invented way of life or some newly concocted religion but to their very being as it was originally intended. The one in whom they believe is the Word who was in the beginning, and

**Close With a
Celebration of the ■
Creative Word**

Think of some of your favorite things, and then cry out loud: "And God said, 'Let there be _____.' " These could be all sorts of things, great and small, such as roses, grandchildren, faith, chocolate, and so on. Close this celebration of creation with the hymn of Francis of Assisi, "All Creatures of Our God and King."

through whom all things were made. They are now made "children of God," true; but that is precisely what they were from the beginning.

The call to follow Jesus and become a child of God is different in time from the call into existence; but its content is the same. Thus, although throughout this book we shall be studying different aspects of Jesus' call, in the end that call is an invitation to become what we were intended to be at that primal call, when of each one of us the eternal Word of God said, "Let there be . . . !"

Session Two

Jesus Calls Into Discipleship

Session Focus ■

This session deals with the calling of the first four disciples. We begin at this point, because this is what immediately comes to mind when we say that "Jesus calls." As we study this passage, we shall see that the call to Peter and the other disciples is not as abrupt as we often think. Indeed, we shall see that "the call" is often a series of calls, each built on a response to previous ones.

Session Objective ■

To understand that the call from Jesus is not always a dramatic call to something unusual or heroic. It may come as a series of calls to be heeded in minor steps just as much as in a dramatic call that requires heroic obedience. The objective is also to explore how obedience in the apparently lesser calls can prepare us for obedience in the more difficult ones.

Session Preparation ■

Compare Luke 5:1-11 with the parallel passages in Matthew 4:18-22 and Mark 1:16-20.

(Luke 5:1-11)

The Call of the Disciples

This is the story of the calling of the first disciples. You are probably more familiar with the way it is told in Mark 1:16-20. Mark tends to limit his narrative to the bare bones. In this case, he simply tells us that Jesus saw Simon and Andrew fishing, told them to follow him, and they did. He adds that "as he went a little farther," he saw James and John and called them. They too followed him. Matthew takes the story from Mark and retells it almost word for word (Matthew 4:18-22) with practically no explanation.

A Baffling Story

That "bare bones" narrative has baffled me ever since I first heard it in Sunday school. I had repeatedly been told to beware of strangers. If a stranger told me to come with him or her, I was told that I should refuse. Yet in this case Jesus appears, apparently as a stranger to Peter, Andrew, John, and James. He invites the four to follow him, and they do. I found particularly puzzling the final word at the end of the story that John and James left their father. My parents would not have been too pleased if I suddenly left them to go away with a stranger!

Prepare small strips of paper and pen or pencils for the final act of worship.

Prepare the story lines described in "A Strange Response to Success" (pages 25–27) to give out to participants.

If you have access to art books, find paintings of the miracle of the great catch of fish. Place them in appropriate places in your learning area so that participants may see them as they arrive.

Choose from among these activities and discussion starters to plan your lesson.

A Baffling Story ■

What do you remember about Peter's call into discipleship? Did you experience difficulties with Peter's call similar to the difficulties that the author of the study describes? Did it ever seem too abrupt? Why or why not?

As I grew up, some of the puzzlement began to subside. Obviously, Peter and the rest were grown men, capable of deciding for themselves and ready to leave their homes, as people generally do as they mature. On that score at least, my mind was set at ease. But there was still the question of these four apparently busy men being ready to leave everything behind on no more than the word of a stranger. I remember making a comment to that effect to my pastor, and his immediate response was that the power of Jesus' personality was such that they simply had to follow. According to my pastor, Jesus simply exuded such an aura of truth and authority that people had no choice but to trust him. Quite frankly, I did not find that explanation very convincing.

Apparently Luke had similar problems with the story as Mark and Matthew told it. His account is fuller, and makes it clear that Jesus did not simply appear, so to speak, "out of the blue," telling these four to follow him. According to Luke's account, Jesus was already a rather well-known teacher, with crowds "pressing in on him to hear the word of God." When we read this, and go back to the story as Mark and Matthew tell it, we realize that, with fewer words, they give us a similar background. Both Mark and Luke tell us that Jesus had been preaching in Galilee—they just do not expand on it. In fact, part of the problem is that we tend not to read the story as a whole, but rather to begin simply with the moment Peter appears on the scene. According to Mark and Matthew, Jesus had already been preaching and teaching in the region—apparently for some time—before he called Peter and the rest. He did not come to them as a complete stranger.

Luke's Account

Read Luke 5:1-11. What implications do you see in the fact that Peter had just taken Jesus out on his boat so that Jesus could speak to the crowd? What does this detail say about Peter's acquaintance with Jesus' teachings?

Luke's Account

Luke develops the narrative further, so that the call comes to Peter and the rest through a series of steps. First of all, they must have been part of the crowd that was gathered beside the lake. (The "lake of Gennesaret" is just a different name for the "sea of Galilee.") This crowd was eager to hear the word of God from Jesus. So, at the very least, we know that Peter and the rest had some idea of who Jesus was, and what some of the claims were that circulated about him.

Then Jesus got into Peter's boat and asked him to put out into the lake, so he could use the boat as a speaking platform to address the crowd. By the time Jesus finished speaking, Peter had heard and seen him up close, and had some idea of what Jesus taught.

Now Jesus made an even stranger demand on Peter. He told Peter, who was a professional fisherman, to try fishing according to the instructions of Jesus, who may have been a famous teacher but who, after all, was a carpenter, and no expert in fishing. Once again, Peter complied. The result was a catch so abundant that Peter and his crew had to call on their partners in the other boat—presumably John and James—to help them pull the nets in. By then, Peter was overwhelmed. Not only had he heard rumors and stories of Jesus and his teachings and deeds. Now he has heard him teach personally and has become a witness and even a participant in one of those deeds. His reaction is one of awe and fear: "Go away from me, Lord, for I am a sinful man!" It is at this point that Jesus told him that he had other plans for Peter; he would now be fishing no longer for fish but for people. It is only after all these events that Peter and the rest left their boats and nets in order to follow Jesus.

As Luke tells it, the story is easier to understand than the story as Mark and Matthew tell it. Jesus was no stranger. Nor did he call Simon to follow him the moment they met. There were a series of steps, and through them—and later through a series of other steps that Luke recounts as his story unfolds—Simon the fisherman will become Peter the fisher of people, or Peter the apostle.

This is important for us, because one of the ways in which we often avoid heeding the call of Jesus is by claiming that he has not called us with the authority by which he called Peter and the rest. If he would only call us in like manner, we surely would follow! When I was a teenager in the Methodist Youth Fellowship, one of our favorite religious poems was by a famous Mexican poet who declared himself ready to leave everything behind in order to follow Jesus; but he wanted a clear call, one that would break through his doubts and his desires. With such a call, he would leave everything and devote his life to following Jesus. As we read this poem in our youth group, we all felt inspired and edified. It is now many decades later that I have come to realize that what that poet was doing, and what we in our youth group were doing, was blaming Jesus for our unwillingness to follow. If we only had a clearer call, we would certainly follow! But, since we do not have it, we may continue along our merry way, telling Jesus that, if he really wants us, he should call louder!

Luke's story makes it more difficult for us to think in those terms. Jesus does not suddenly call Peter to a heroic leaving of his boat and nets. Before such a call, Peter has heard and obeyed his call in other ways— some of them less dramatic than the act of leaving the nets. First, Peter was part of a crowd that had heard at least the call to come and listen. Then, he had obeyed Jesus when asked to put out into the lake and lent his boat to serve as a speaking platform for Jesus. Having done that, and having seen and heard Jesus up close, he was even willing to obey the apparently absurd instruction from a carpenter to a fisherman as to where to cast his nets.

Each of these steps requires a different measure of commitment. Each of them is difficult to conceive without the previous one. If Peter had not been amidst a crowd that was eager to see and hear Jesus, he would have had no reason to agree to the request from Jesus to put out into the lake. If he had not been already out on the lake, and had not seen and heard Jesus teach, he probably would not have cast his nets as Jesus told him to do. If he had not cast his nets, he would not have been awed by the power and authority of Jesus in contrast to his own sinfulness. Only after all of these steps in obedience were Peter and his companions ready to leave their nets, their boats, and even their families, and follow Jesus.

The same is true of us. If I had really waited for Jesus to call me as that favorite Mexican poet of my youth demanded, I would still be repeating that poem and waiting for my first call!

Step by Step ■

An ancient custom in many churches, now often left behind, is to give "testimonies" of the work of God in our own lives. How does your own calling illustrate the manner in which one call has led to another, and then to another?

Step by Step

Look at Paul's calling. We often tell the story of his experience on the road to Damascus. That was certainly a life-changing experience. Yet, that was not the last call that Paul received. On the road to Damascus, he was simply told to continue to Damascus and there to await instructions. When those instructions finally came by means of Ananias, they were limited. Paul was simply called to become a Christian. Later he was in his native region of Cilicia when the Lord used Barnabas to call him to ministry in Antioch. Once Paul had worked in Antioch and become a leader in that church, the Spirit told the believers to set aside both Paul and Barnabas for a particular task. From that point on, there was a series of new calls, such as the vision of the young Macedonian who told him, "Come to Macedonia and help us."

Both Peter and Paul received further calls as they obeyed and followed previous ones, and the same is true of just about every Christian. The Lord will not call us to step five if we balk at step one. If, on the other hand, we heed and obey the call to step one, there will be a call to step two. And if we obey that call, there will be another call to step three. And so on.

What all of this means for us today is that we must take care lest the illusion that we would be faithful under extraordinary and heroic circumstances keep us from being faithful in the ordinary events and calls of our daily life.

It also means that, as we obey in the apparently lesser calls that come to us in daily life, we shall become more attuned to the Lord's will, and therefore will be ready to heed other calls that otherwise we would not even have imagined.

Calling and Training ■

Read 1 Corinthians 9:24-27 and Hebrews 12:1-3. What do these passages say to you about calling and its similarity to athletic training?

Calling and Training

Preparing for the calls of Jesus is like training for a sport. It is by practicing that we become able to perform greater and better deeds. A runner does not go into a marathon without spending many other hours running shorter races. Each of those other runs builds on the earlier ones, and they all prepare the runner for the greater challenge. The same is true with the calls of Jesus and our obedience to them.

A Strange Response to Success ■

Form two teams and assign a storyline to each:
Storyline 1: You are a farmer. This year your land has yielded its highest ever. Your harvest is about to sell at record prices.
Storyline 2: You are a farmer. This year your land has been so devastated by drought and blight that it has yielded no harvest at all.
Each team will read Luke 5 1-11, then discuss the following question: When you consider your team's storyline, what do you find interesting or attractive in this Scripture? Tell the main points of your conversation to the entire group.

A Strange Response to Success

Another interesting aspect of this story in Luke is Peter's reaction to the miraculous catch. He and his companions had spent all night fishing and caught nothing. As fishermen, they had failed—at least for the time being. Their career was not at its high point. Now, with just one casting of the nets, they had caught more fish than they normally would have in many days and nights of fishing. A short while before, they had been at least temporary failures in their careers. Now their success was astonishing. If Peter were to follow some of the preaching we hear today, he would have said: "Look! If you follow Jesus, you prosper in your career. You certainly catch more fish!" But his reaction was just the opposite. He recognized that what had happened was a sign of the power and authority of Jesus. And the moment he recognized this he was led to acknowledge his own unworthiness: "Go away from me, Lord, for I am a sinful man!" The presence of God's power was overwhelming to such a point that the fish were no longer important. Quite clearly, such an enormous catch would have been an economic boon to Peter and his companions. But Peter, rather than saying, "Thank you, Jesus. Keep the blessings coming!" says "I am a sinful man!" Before the glory of the Almighty, all else becomes secondary, and all we can do is confess our unworthiness and cry out for forgiveness.

A blessing—any blessing—is a two-edged

reality. It certainly does us good. It may grant us a boon that we really desire; but it also places us face-to-face with the Almighty, and that is an awe-inspiring experience! A blessing is not just a prayer answered, or a sign of God's love. A blessing is also a sign of the awesome and overwhelming presence of God. A blessing makes us feel loved and cared for; but it also reminds us of our own unworthiness and sinfulness. If it is truly a blessing coming from the grace of God—and not just something we think we have earned or deserve—it leads us to a response akin to Peter's: "I am a sinful man!"

Yet, there is another dimension to this episode that merits our attention. Peter decided to leave his nets and follow Jesus, not because his business had failed but rather at the point of his greatest business success. In today's terms, we would say that he was at the pinnacle of his career. He decides to follow Jesus, not because he has tried his hand at fishing and failed, but because he has achieved a success that he knows he does not deserve, a success that is not of his own doing.

Quite often we hear stories of people who were "at the end of their rope," or "down and out." They had come to a point of absolute despair and hopelessness. They saw no way out, and at that point they gave their lives to Jesus. That is a common, true, and valid experience. But we must not forget that there is also the experience of coming to Jesus, not out of failure but out of success. In the fourth century, Ambrose was a successful government official when he was called to lead the church in Milan. In the thirteenth century, Francis was the well-to-do son of a successful merchant when he decided to follow Jesus by joining the ranks of the poor and devoting his life to service and to preaching. In the nineteenth century, Albert Schweitzer was an acclaimed physician, theologian, and organist when he received the call to serve the sick in Africa. Today, you may be at the very top of your career. Even so, the Lord may be calling you to unexpected adventures in obedience!

Calling and Occupation

Note then the connection between Peter's previous occupation and his new calling: "from now on you will be catching people"—or, as other translations say, "fishing for people." This is more than just a nice turn of phrase. Peter the fisherman will still fish. Somehow his previous experience fishing in the sea of Galilee will help him as he fishes for people in the wider world. The past is not to be forgotten, totally abandoned, or obliterated. His calling and his previous career somehow connect. What he learned as he fished for fish will serve him as he fishes for people.

Because conversion is such a radical experience that it is akin to being born anew, too often people think that there has to be an absolute discontinuity between the "before" and the "after" of Christian discipleship. Certainly, there is much that will have to be abandoned or changed. But there will still be continuity. Somehow, the Lord will not only redeem us for a future life with him. The Lord also redeems our past—even our past apart from him. The Lord uses all that we know, all that we have experienced, and all that we are, and calls us to put all of that at his disposal.

At this point, it is helpful to bring to mind the connection between *calling* and *vocation*. In some cases we use these two words as

Calling and Occupation ■

On a scale from 1 to 10 silently evaluate your own occupation according to (1) how much good you do and (2) how good you feel doing it. After some time for reflection and prayer, consider the following questions: How does the understanding of your occupation as a vocation, or call from God, change your perspective about your work? What connections do you see between survival, occupation, and vocation? How might people who must work to survive fulfill a "vocation," or call from God?

interchangeable synonyms. Thus, we may say that our calling is to be a lawyer, or a painter, or a poet. Indeed, the very word vocation comes from the Latin *vocatio*, which means "calling." In the best of cases, our occupation is a calling from God. It is then a true vocation, a true *vocatio*, and not just something we do because we enjoy doing it or because we are good at it. In other cases, our occupation may be something God will use for our further calling—as in the case of Peter, whose occupation as a fisherman became the starting point for his calling as a disciple and an apostle. But if we see no connection between our occupation and our calling from Jesus, no way in which our occupation may be connected with our vocation in that higher sense, it may be time for us to begin considering a radical change in our way of life.

How do you know if your occupation is also a vocation, a call from God? There are two important indicators: (1) how much good you do, and (2) how good you feel in doing it. A true vocation from God matches both what the world needs and what you are good at. God will not call you to do something absolutely useless or something that is absolutely contrary to the abilities and inclinations that God has placed on you.

Hearing the Call and Leaving the Nets Behind

Now we finally come to the point that is most often stressed when studying the call of the first disciples: what they left behind. The point is made often that when Jesus called them, these first disciples were willing to leave behind their boats, their nets, and even the father of two of them, Zebedee.

(Actually, Luke speaks only of Peter, and at the end of the story says "they" followed him, without specifying who "they" are. We know that they are Peter's brother Andrew and Zebedee's two sons, John and James, because Matthew and Mark say so.) This is held up as a great example of the sacrifices that a life of discipleship requires. This is indeed so, and in another session we shall deal with such sacrifices and self-denial.

However, as part of the background to understand this lesson, it is helpful to remember that every decision implies leaving behind possibilities and options that are no longer available. Likewise, all growth implies leaving something behind. Paul reminds us that when one is a child, one thinks as a child; but when one matures, one leaves childish things behind. That is not always easy to understand or to accept. I still remember how I cried when Bambi grew up to the point of being separated from his mother. I wished that he could somehow grow up to be a powerful stag, and yet remain the same Bambi that I had come to love. But it was not possible. If this is true of all growth, it is equally true of growth in discipleship—or of any process of following Jesus.

This idea implies that heeding any call from Jesus implies leaving some things behind. Think of it. When Peter and his companions decided to listen to Jesus as he came to the lakeshore, they had to give up the option of going home, or whatever else they could have done. When Peter agreed to take Jesus out in his boat, he gave up some of his authority over his own boat. It is not just the dramatic act of leaving the nets and boats that implies leaving something behind. Every choice is precisely that: a saying "yes" to something and therefore "no" to something else.

Once again, this is why it is so important

to heed the call of Jesus in little and seemingly simple or "unimportant" circumstances, and not wait for the heroic moments. When Peter agreed to take Jesus out into the lake, he began to relinquish authority over his boat. When he agreed to cast his nets, he began to relinquish authority over those nets. His leaving behind boat and nets, dramatic as it is, does not happen without previous steps whereby he is being prepared for the drastic decision that he is to make.

That is what was wrong about the poem that my youth group loved so much. We did not realize that every time Jesus called us to do something, no matter how small or how simple, we were taking steps toward more difficult decisions—difficult in part because they would require greater self-denial. Jesus calls us, not just once to some great deed but repeatedly to ever more challenging levels of discipleship. If we are not willing to respond to the simplest calls, to those that require less sacrifice, we shall hardly be ready for the more difficult ones.

Session Three

Jesus Calls by Naming and Renaming

Session Focus ■

"Calling" is also naming. In this passage, Simon names Jesus the Messiah, and Jesus names Peter the Rock. When Jesus calls us, he also invites us to name him. What we name him— what we see in him—is crucial for our discipleship, for calling is much like a conversation in which we name Jesus and he in turn names us.

Session Objective ■

To become aware that the form of our discipleship greatly depends on our view of Jesus, and to study the life and teachings of Jesus in order to explore who it is we are called to be.

Session Preparation ■

Look up in a Bible dictionary some of these terms: *Son of man, Messiah, Christ, Joshua, salvation.* Have a large piece of paper or a chalkboard available to write words that people will suggest. Review what we studied earlier about the meaning of names and their importance.

(Matthew 16:13-20)

A Dangerous Confession

Most interpreters are agreed that Matthew 16:13-20 is one of the main turning points in the Gospel narratives. We who now read these narratives know that part of the point of the story is precisely that Jesus is the Christ, the son of the loving God. But Peter and the disciples had not been told before. They had seen many signs that there was something special about Jesus. Peter himself had been a participant in the miraculous catch of fish and a witness to many other such events. One may well imagine that they wondered who Jesus was and what was the source of his power and wisdom. Matthew tells us that some time earlier Jesus had stilled the storm; and the disciples, amazed, had asked themselves: "What sort of man is this, that even the winds and the sea obey him?" (Matthew 8:27). Since at that point Jesus did not tell them, there must have been many such conversations among them.

It is at this point, in the district of Caesarea Philippi, that the question is finally answered. Up to this time, the disciples may have wondered if they were following an exceptional teacher or a very powerful miracle worker. But after this day, they now knew that Jesus is the Christ, the Messiah.

This knowledge had many implications, even beyond its obvious religious consequences. The Messiah, the Christ, or the Anointed One (*Christ* is the Greek form of the Hebrew *Messiah*, which means "Anointed") was expected to restore the throne of David. Since at that time Jerusalem and all of Judea were under Roman rule, any attempt at such Davidic restoration would be seen as subversive by Roman authorities, as well as by those Jewish authorities who ruled the land in Rome's behalf and who were subservient to the power of Rome. We usually do not think that Christian faith is subversive. But for many Christians living under conditions of oppression, it clearly is. In the time of Jesus, to claim to be the Messiah was both subversive and dangerous. Remember that eventually Jesus was crucified by the Romans, precisely under the accusation of having claimed to be "King of the Jews," that is, of attempting to restore the throne of David and claiming it for himself. The Romans did not look with favor on such pretensions.

"Who Do People Say That the Son of Man Is?"

At any rate, the conversation begins as a question of identity. Jesus is aware that people are talking about him, and he asks his disciples about the opinions that are circulating about his own identity. The title of "Son of Man" is one of the ways in which Jesus refers to himself in the Gospels. It is not a way of saying that he is human, as a sort of counterpart to being "Son of God." It was actually a title that appeared in earlier Jewish literature, including the Book of Daniel (7:13). It was a somewhat unclear title given to a figure whose coming would signal God's

Choose from among these activities and discussion starters to plan your lesson.

"Who Do People Say That the Son of Man Is?"

Read Matthew 16:13-20. Look up *Son of man* in a good Bible dictionary such as *The Interpreter's Dictionary of the Bible.* Look up *Messiah* and *Christ.* How do these articles inform your understanding of the Scripture?

Invite the group to place themselves in a number of roles. Some can be Roman soldiers, occupying Palestine and being keenly aware that they are not popular. Others can be the high priest, or Herod, or a tax collector. All of these serve at the pleasure of the Roman Empire. Invite them to consider how they might react to hearing that someone is going around claiming to be the promised Messiah, who will fulfill the promises made to Israel. How would they react to such news? (Hint: Look at John 11:47-50 and 12:9-11.)

intervention. Since "Son of Man" was not as clearly defined as the title of Messiah, Jesus calls himself by this title in the Gospels as a way of indicating that he is extraordinary but without openly claiming the role of the Messiah or Christ—until this moment in the narrative.

The opinions about Jesus that the disciples report are varied. Clearly it was commonly held that Jesus was no ordinary man. Notice that apparently all the opinions circulating about him suggested that he was a prophet who had returned—John the Baptist, who had been beheaded shortly before; Elijah, who had been carried away into heaven; or Jeremiah or some other prophet, all long since dead. Clearly, the teachings and deeds of Jesus were such that some extraordinary explanation must be found. On this point all seem to agree.

The debate about who Jesus is goes beyond a point of curiosity. If Jesus is John the Baptist, he will be expected to act in a certain way. If he is Elijah, his actions will be different. In seeking to name Jesus people were trying to peg down his mission and its result. Once again, we are reminded of the connection between naming and calling. When people seek to name Jesus, they are actually calling him—expecting him—to do certain things and not others.

Who Do You Say That I Am?

Jesus then asked them the question point blank. It is easy to report the opinion of others. It is much more difficult to commit to a personal opinion or view. Whatever other people thought about Jesus would affect the disciples only indirectly. But what they thought about him would affect them directly and personally.

The one who answered was Simon, the fisherman whose initial calling we studied in the last session. His words are astonishing: "You are the Messiah [or the Christ], the Son of the living God." Again, these were daring words not only in religious terms but also in their practical consequences. If Jesus were, as common opinion apparently held, a prophet who had returned, he could be calling the people to a new obedience and to repentance, as did John the Baptist. This could lead to conflict with corrupt leaders who would resent such a call to righteousness and repentance. Indeed, John the Baptist had been imprisoned and beheaded precisely for those reasons. If he were Elijah, he would be seen as a forerunner, an announcement, of the coming of the Messiah. This would lead to even greater difficulties, for now he would not be a challenge only to corrupt local politicians such as Herod but to the Roman Empire itself, whose power would have to be curtailed if the throne of David was to be restored. But if he were the Messiah, the Anointed One, the challenge to the authorities would be greater and direct. In that case, he was not just an announcement of a new order. He was the leader and the founder of that new order. He was not just saying that the long-awaited time was coming soon; he was bringing that time about.

Thus, for Peter to declare, "You are the Christ," was a bold act of commitment to a heady and dangerous expectation. Peter was saying that the time had come for the vindication of the people of God, for the fulfillment of God's promises. One could even say that he was declaring that he was following a leader who would bring about a new order—and the only way to do this was to clash with the existing order, namely, the Roman Empire and its minions in Jerusalem.

Peter named Jesus as "the Christ" (or the Messiah). In so doing, he not only gave Jesus a title; he also proclaimed what he considered to be Jesus' calling. In those few words, Peter set forth an entire plan of action for Jesus—a plan that Peter thought was determined by what the calling of the Messiah would be.

Significantly, if in our previous session we saw Jesus calling Peter, now we find Peter calling Jesus—calling him the Messiah, the Son of the living God.

You Are Peter

Jesus began by affirming what Peter had just said. He even declared that Peter's affirmation was not the result of "flesh and blood"—that is, of human proof or reasoning—but of a direct revelation from God. Peter may have seen many wonders and heard words of profound wisdom; but even all of this would never suffice to bring him to the conviction that Jesus is the Christ. Faith does not come from proof—even by the proof of the most astounding miracles—but by the action and revelation of God.

Now Jesus responded by his own act of naming, which in itself is also an act of calling. He had just used Simon's full name, "Simon, son of Jonah." Now he gave Simon a different name, the name by which posterity would remember him: "And I tell you, you are Peter, and on this rock I will build my church."

To understand this passage it is important to realize that what we have here is a play on words. Although the New Testament was written in Greek, Jesus most probably was

You Are Peter ■

What does the name "the rock" suggest to you about personal characteristics? How do you think Peter reflects or lives out the name given to him by Jesus? How does he fall short of the name? In what ways would knowing Jesus and naming Jesus as Messiah give depth and meaning to the name "the rock"?

speaking Aramaic. In Aramaic, *rock* is "cephas." This is why in some passages in the New Testament, Peter is called Cephas. Simon's new name, in Greek, is "Petros." In Greek, a rock is "petra." Thus, Simon's new name is the masculine form of "rock," and what Jesus was saying is, "You are Rock, and on this rock I will build my church." (Unfortunately, due to anti-Catholic polemics, many Protestant interpreters have claimed that the "rock" is not Peter, but his confession. We would all do better were we to read this passage apart from later attempts to base papal supremacy on it. While it is true that the church is built on Peter's confession, this particular text clearly calls Peter, and not his confession, "Rock.")

In brief, when Simon named Jesus the Christ, Jesus responded by naming Peter the Rock. Naming Jesus (declaring who he is and who he is called to be) is not just an outward matter of opinion; it also rebounds on the one doing the naming. If Simon declared that Jesus is the Messiah, Jesus now declares that Simon is the rock of his new movement. If Simon's declaration was heady and dangerous, he is now given an appropriately heady and dangerous task. I can well imagine Simon, now Peter, reflecting on the conversation that has just taken place. He has declared that Jesus will lead the movement that will restore the throne of David, and now he finds himself up to his neck in the glories and dangers of such an expectation. I can also imagine that Peter was greatly relieved when Jesus ordered his disciples not to tell anyone that he was the Messiah. The moment of danger and decision is mercifully postponed.

We who know the story know also that Peter was no rock. He was impulsive and anything *but* firm as a rock. In a moment we shall see him wavering. Later he would deny even knowing Jesus. And yet, Jesus calls him Rock. Eventually he does become a rock. Remember that, as we saw in our first session, the one who names Peter Rock is the same Word who was in the beginning, and at whose utterance all things were made. This is the Word that says, "Let there be . . . ," and there is. If this Word says that Peter is Rock, a rock he will be.

A New Name?

The question that Jesus asked of his disciples in the district of Caesarea Philippi he has asked of his followers through the ages, and still asks today. This is not just a matter of what we shall name him. It is also a matter of what he will name us, what he will call us to do. Next session, as we study the continuation of today's passage, we shall see that Jesus soon began helping Peter redefine what the declaration, "you are the Christ," really meant, and how that also involved a clarification of the meaning of being Peter, the Rock.

There are many examples along the history of the church of how who we say Jesus is has an impact on how we seek to serve Jesus, and therefore has an impact on who we are. In the early church, when Christians were demeaned by society and persecuted by the state, they saw Jesus as both the priestly king who had made them a royal priesthood (1 Peter 2:9; Revelation 1:5) and the one who had conquered death by dying (1 Corinthians 15:55-56; Ephesians 4:8-10), who thereby was a witness to a different kind of

A New Name? ■
Look around at the other members of the group. Think of new names for them that reflect what you see as their Christian traits or virtues. These could be real traditional names such as *Faith, Hope,* or *Peter.* Or they could be words that somehow reflect that person's gifts, such as *Faithful, Generous, Trustworthy,* and so forth. Write these names on small pieces of paper and give them to the person you are "renaming."

victory (Revelation 1:5). In consequence, these believers whom society demeaned saw themselves as children and heirs of the great King, and this in turn gave them power and stamina to withstand all the humiliations and evil gossip to which they were subjected. In ancient times, many Christians took a new name at the time of their baptism, as an indication of the new reality into which they were being called, of their new birth and their new life. Fishmongers, slaves, cooks, and oppressed wives now had a new, hidden name, a different reality. They were children of the Most High. This was a dignity no one could take away from them.

Likewise, when brought before the courts, tortured, and condemned to death, they remembered that their Lord had conquered through the cross, and they saw their sufferings as part of God's great victory, in which they were given a chance to participate, and in which Christ suffered with them.

Then the growing church had to venture out into the world of ideas and of knowledge. This was, as it has always been, a harshly competitive world, in which Christian doctrine was often mocked and rejected. Many believers simply responded by a similar rejection, declaring that all such knowledge was at best worthless, and perhaps even inspired by evil demons. But there were other Christians who remembered that this Christ whom they worshiped was the Word through whom all things were made, the light that illumines every human being, and on that basis those Christians felt called to show the connection between the gospel and the best of human wisdom.

Much later, in the thirteenth century, when a sudden explosion in wealth and trade threatened to dehumanize society and when violence had become a way of life in Western Europe, there was a young man, the son of a wealthy merchant, who saw Jesus as the peace-loving and peace-making teacher who gave up his career as a carpenter in order to live as a poor beggar wandering along the countryside preaching peace and love. And so Francis felt called to give up his father's wealth, to renounce violence, and to live as a poor beggar preaching peace and love, even to the much feared and hated Sultan of Egypt.

Still later, in the twentieth century, there was a young woman who saw Jesus as the one who, according to his promise, comes to us in the poor, the hungry, and the naked. And thus Mother Theresa went to India.

These are a few of the many notable examples of Christians who in the very act of calling Jesus—of responding to the question "Who do you say that I am?"—were themselves called. Yet let us not be derailed by the exceptional. What was true of the early martyrs, of Francis of Assisi, and of Mother Theresa has also been true of every common and unnamed Christian throughout history. It should also be true of each one of us.

Your Own Name ■

In the light of the earlier discussion about the meaning of names, do you think your own name gives any sort of hint as to who or what you should be? If Jesus were responding to you as he did to Simon, how might he change or redefine your name?

Bible 301 ☐

A common mistake: It is often said that after his

Your Own Name

Then, we must also be aware that naming Jesus by the wrong name—seeing him as what he is not—can also lead to terrible aberrations in Christian practice. In the next session we shall see Simon Peter trying to redefine the mission of Jesus, and being rebuked as an agent of Satan. Too often Christians have answered the question, "Who do you say that I am?" by declaring Jesus to be a mighty warrior who is willing to crush his enemies by the power of arms, and conversion Saul became Paul. While it is true that name changes are important, in the case of Paul his two names had nothing to do with his conversion. Note that in Acts, even after his conversion, he is still Saul, and that he becomes Paul only in Chapter 13 at the beginning of the mission to the Gentiles. Paul, like many other Jews at the time, had a Jewish name (Saul, the only king of Israel from Paul's own tribe of Benjamin), and a Latin name that they used in the outside world, which often was similar to their Jewish name. Thus, Saul takes the name of Paul, and Silas becomes Silvanus, when they are in a non-Jewish context.

Naming Jesus ■

Think of one-word descriptions of who and how you think Jesus is. You might think of words such as "savior," "powerful," "loving," "just," and so forth. Write these words on a large sheet of paper or on a chalkboard. What do these descriptions of Jesus imply for our own discipleship today? In other words, if this is who Jesus is, who and what are we supposed to be?
(Look at Session Four. If you will use this list for that session, save it.)

Bible 301 □

Jesus is the same name as Joshua, and it means "God

as a result they have felt called to set off crusades against those whom they considered the enemies of Jesus, those who usually turned out to be the same as the enemies of those Christians. Or they have considered Jesus to be a stickler for "true doctrine," and then they have felt called to uproot every vestige of error, sometimes even by burning it in the person of "heretics." Or they have turned Jesus into the guardian of common decency and morality, and then they have conceived their calling as scrutinizing other people's lives, to see if they live by "Christian" standards. Or they have therefore decided that Jesus loves the church and hates the rest of the world, and they have convinced themselves that their task is simply to build up the church and let the world follow its own path to destruction.

Naming Jesus

Calling is very much like a conversation: it is a two-way relationship. Obviously, in that relationship the followers of Jesus are not his equals. As we saw in our very first session, the Word of God calls us into existence. Therefore, the relationship is not symmetric. Still, there is always a conversation. Jesus calls us, and that call we can hear because it comes with power—much as it came to Simon, to whom it was not revealed by flesh or blood but by God. At the same time, however, in responding to his call we also call or name him; we have a view of who he is and what he is to do. He tells us what we are to be, and we hear that call on the basis of who we believe he is. It is for this reason that the call, like a good conversation, does not end but is constantly renewed and clarified. We shall see a concrete example of this in our saves" or "God is salvation." Look back at Matthew 1:21, where the Lord tells Joseph that the child to be born will be named Jesus, and why. You may wish to remind the group of what was said earlier about the process and the importance of naming a child; then reflect on how the very name Jesus already tells us something about his place in God's plan. For this discussion, it may help to remember that in the Bible "salvation" is much more than going to heaven. Look up that word in a Bible dictionary.

A Closing Prayer ■

Pray: "You are the Christ, the Son of the living God. Tell me, who am I in your sight?" After a moment of silence, listen for an answer, then repeat the same prayer. After three or four such repetitions, close with the Lord's Prayer.

next session, where we shall be studying the continuation of the passage we have studied today.

Meanwhile, however, consider the question, Who do you think Jesus is? In so doing, you will be considering your own calling.

Session Four

Jesus Calls Into Death and Life

Session Focus ■

In this session we shall be looking at the cross of Jesus and its significance in shaping our discipleship. Jesus calls us to take up the cross. What does this mean? What does it mean in a society where the very meaning of the cross as a symbol has changed, from a secular instrument of torture and death to a religious symbol?

Session Objective ■

To reflect on Jesus' invitation to take up the cross and follow him, to know that this is not so much a call to a single act of obedience as it is a call to a different way of life, and to learn that the self-denial for which Jesus calls is a joy-producing self-denial in which one finds the self that would otherwise be lost.

Session Preparation ■

Read Matthew 16:21-26; Isaiah 42:1-4; 49:1-6; 50:4-9; 52:13–53:12; 1 Peter 2:21-25. Make a list of some of the ways in which the group characterized Jesus toward the end of the last session.

(Matthew 16:21-26)

This passage is the continuation of the one we studied in Session Three. In some of our Bibles, this may be obscured by subheadings that have been introduced into the text, dividing it into two different sections. While such subheadings facilitate our reading, sometimes they hide the connection between passages that are in fact the continuation of each other. In this case, it is important that we see the connection between the conversation in Caesarea Philippi and what we are now told.

That connection is indicated by the very first words of our text for today, "From that time on, Jesus began. . . ." In other words, it was only after Peter had declared him to be the Messiah, and Jesus had confirmed this declaration and told his disciples to keep it secret, that Jesus began telling them of the horrible events that awaited him in Jerusalem.

The Messiah Redefined

What Jesus is in fact doing is redefining and clarifying what being the Messiah actually means. The most commonly held notion by those who awaited the coming of the Messiah was that he would be a conquering hero who would lead a military uprising

Write or recruit someone to write Peter's explanation of his attitude several days before the group meets.

Choose from among these activities and discussion starters to plan your lesson.

The Messiah Redefined ■

Read the main "Songs of the Suffering Servant": Isaiah 42:1-4; 49:1-6; 50:4-9; 52:13–53:12. Look at 1 Peter 2:21-25, which makes the suffering of Jesus a pattern for our own calling. What insights do you gain from these Scriptures about the meaning of *Messiah*? about Jesus' understanding of his role as Messiah? What connections can you make between these Scriptures and what it means to live as Christians in the contemporary world?

against the forces of occupation, and set his throne in Jerusalem. Obviously, there would be a struggle. But in that struggle the Messiah, like David of old, would conquer his enemies.

There were, however, other ways of understanding the task of the Messiah. Particularly in the Book of Isaiah, there was a series of songs about the "Suffering Servant" (see Isaiah 42:1-4; 49:1-6; 50:4-9; 52:13–53:12). Note that sometimes these passages were applied to Israel itself, as God's suffering people. They were applied to Jesus from a very early time. In a way, then, they should also be applied to the church, who as the people of the Suffering Servant must also be a people who overcome enemies, not with violence or with raw power but with love. The best known of the Suffering Servant Scriptures is found in Isaiah 53, which you may wish to read. The Suffering Servant was a paradoxical figure who suffered not because of his sins but for the sins of others. He was sent by God to do God's will and to conquer in God's name. But his victory was not like the victories of the kings of the earth and their military leaders. On the contrary, he would conquer by suffering.

Thus, what Jesus began to do as soon as Peter declared him to be the Messiah and he accepted the title was to clarify what it meant. Jesus will be a Messiah like the Suffering Servant, and not like a conquering general. He must go to Jerusalem, not to claim the throne or to expel the Romans and their minions, but to suffer at the hands of the religious leaders of his own people—"the elders and chief priests and scribes." He would conquer not just the Romans and the leaders of Jerusalem who lent themselves to the service of Rome but death itself. Yet, he would conquer death by submitting to it, by allowing the powers of evil to take hold of him and do their very worst, and then rising on the third day.

Peter's Objections ■

A few days before the session, write a letter, as if it were Peter writing to a later disciple (for instance, Mark), trying to explain how he felt when Jesus began saying that he must go to Jerusalem and be crucified. Read the letter to the group.

Peter's Objections

We, who know the story and have read it a hundred times, find it difficult to understand Peter's objections. We look at the story from this side of Easter and Pentecost, and after 20 centuries of preaching and interpretation, we are surprised that Peter, who had just confessed Jesus to be the Messiah, can be so troubled by what Jesus announced.

Try to place yourself in Peter's situation and listen to the words of Jesus as Peter must have heard them. You have been raised by the sea of Galilee, among people who fish for a living and others whose generally drab and uneventful life is made bearable by the expectation of better days—of days when the throne of David will be restored, when heavy Roman taxation and other forms of exploitation will be a matter of the past. One day you hear of this great teacher. You listen to him. You take him out on the lake in your boat. You hear him teach. You see him do wonders. He invites you to follow him; and you do, not really knowing where you are going. Now, after long acquaintance, you have come to the conclusion that he is the Messiah, the Anointed One so long awaited. He tells you that it is indeed so. Your expectations soar. Not only will the throne of David be restored, but you will be right in the very thick of it! Just wait until Zebedee and all the others who are still fishing on the lake hear of this!

Much as you would like to announce the news, Jesus tells you not to tell anybody. You are probably relieved that the time for confrontation with the existing order has not yet arrived. You also wonder about this imposed secret. What does he intend? How can he take Jerusalem without telling others? That is confusing. But you trust your leader. Perhaps he has developed a strategy and is waiting to build up his forces before he declares himself the Messiah and marches on Jerusalem.

Now matters get worse. He not only tells you to keep silent. He also starts telling you some strange and frightening things. Apparently, although he plans to go to Jerusalem, he does not intend to march on it like a conquering hero. He does not even hope to gain the support of the religious leadership of the nation. On the contrary, he expects these people to deny and persecute him. He even expects to die. What kind of Messiah is this? Jesus is saying that he is a different kind of king. His power is not in his ability to make others suffer, as is the case with most earthly rulers. His power is in his love, in his giving of himself, in his willingness to die for the sake of others.

The Rock Is Now Called Satan ■

The Rock Is Now Called Satan

Look again at the list of one-word descriptions of Jesus and his work that you created in Session Three. Which of those descriptions (or others you might think of) best fit what Peter wants Jesus to do? (For instance, "powerful," "conqueror," "ruler," and so forth.) To which do you think Peter would object? (For instance, "suffering" or "patient.") Which of these descrip-

Peter has heeded the call of Jesus to follow. He has received the revelation of God telling him that Jesus is the Messiah, and therefore the one who called him by the lakeshore he now calls Messiah. But what Jesus is telling him requires a radical shift in his thinking. Again, this shift in thinking is not just a matter of his thinking about Jesus. It is also a matter of his thinking about himself. This Messiah has called him Rock, and has given him a special place in this coming movement that he calls his church. If the Messiah is not as Peter had understood him,

tions do you like best? Which cause you difficulties? Why? What does this say about your view of Jesus? What does it say about the aspects of discipleship you like? that you do not like?

this implies a shift, not only for Jesus but also for Peter himself and his role. Apparently he is not to be the head general in this Messiah's army nor the chief advisor standing beside the throne in Jerusalem. If Jesus redefines his own mission, he is also redefining Peter's.

Therefore, Peter objected. Frankly, so would I. Clearly Peter did not want his Lord to suffer. But he also did not want to be a Rock in that Lord's church. Who would want to be a leader of a movement that begins by announcing its defeat? How does one lead in such a movement?

Peter's objections were aimed at the very heart of Jesus' own calling. They have to do with the strange strategy of this Anointed One who plans to establish a kingdom by being killed. Like Satan in the desert, Peter is tempting Jesus to follow the easier road to power. But power gained by force will have no authority. It would be just like the power of the Romans and their puppets in Jerusalem. Jesus' calling is to establish a different sort of kingdom—one that is based on a love that gives of itself, rather than on a self-serving force that takes from others.

Thus, Peter's admonitions were an echo of Satan's temptations in the desert, and Jesus now gave Simon a new name. The one whom he had just called Rock he now calls Satan: "Get behind me, Satan!" Simon the Rock can also be Simon the Satan when he seeks to redefine the mission of Jesus.

Fortunately, we know the rest of the story, and therefore know that eventually the Rock prevailed. But this episode stands as a warning to every follower of Jesus since then: The easy path to power and success, even to religious success, is the path of Satan!

Peter the Rock, and Other Rocks ■

Read 1 Peter 2:1-10. What do the images of stones suggest to you? In what ways can you and your church be "living stones" in building the house of God?

Peter the Rock, and Other Rocks

Look at First Peter. Peter is depicted as addressing the church using the image of rocks repeatedly. Jesus is "the stone that the builders rejected," which now "has become the very head of the corner" (1 Peter 2:7). Following this stone, Christians are to be "like living stones," being built into a spiritual house (1 Peter 2:5). There is some debate as to who actually wrote these words attributed to Peter. Yet, no matter who wrote them, they show that the early church believed that the Rock did allow himself to be shaped and strengthened into a real rock, and that this became a paradigm for other believers to follow. Peter is Rock because he has been made such by the Rock of Ages. We, like him, are also stones, made such by the same Rock of Ages, and part of a great building God is creating.

Discipleship Redefined ■

What does the phrase "take up your cross" suggest to you for contemporary discipleship? If each Christian, as a disciple of Jesus, must take the cross, shouldn't the church do the same? What do you think this means? (Remember the Crusades, when the church "took up the cross" in order to launch a series of wars.) Should the church be willing to appear weak and to suffer humiliation? Or should it be concerned with its own prestige and power? Try to find some examples in decisions your local church or your denomination have faced in the recent past.

Discipleship Redefined

Jesus rejects Peter's attempt to redefine him, and then takes the opportunity to redefine for his followers what he is calling them to do. If he is to be the Messiah of the cross, his followers also are to be followers of the cross. He is going to Jerusalem to suffer many things at the hands of the religious leadership and eventually to be killed. To follow him requires taking a similar path: "If any want to become my followers, let them deny themselves and take up their cross and follow me."

This has become such a common saying that it has lost much of its sting. Look at it again from the perspective of people in the Roman Empire in the first century. The cross was not a religious symbol. It was a symbol of painful and shameful death. It was reserved for the worst criminals. There was nothing romantic or beautiful about it. It was not, as the hymn now says, a "wondrous cross." It was an instrument of torture, plain and simple. It was the sign of a condemned criminal.

Now Jesus tells his followers that they must take up their cross. This is a harsh and even ugly invitation. He is calling them to become outcasts, condemned criminals, as he will become. He is telling them that just as his calling is to go to Jerusalem and suffer, so is their calling one of self-denial and suffering.

The invitation to take up the cross is a calling unto death! For that is what the cross is—an instrument of death. To take up the cross and follow means to go to Calvary, there to be crucified.

Not a Matter of Resignation

What are some examples of "resignation" to one's circumstance that are mistakenly viewed as "bearing the cross"? What connections can you make between this teaching and issues of abuse, oppression, or injustice? How might one use or abuse this teaching in such circumstances?

Not a Matter of Resignation

It is important to clarify this point: Taking up the cross is an active decision. It is not simply a matter of accepting whatever evil befalls us. Quite often when visiting people going through various difficulties, I hear the phrase, "I must bear this cross." There is a sense in which this is a truthful statement, for it reminds us that whenever we suffer, for whatever reason, our Lord suffers with us. We do not have a distant God who cannot share in our afflictions, but one who understands the depths of human suffering (Hebrews 4:15).

However, taking up the cross is much more than simply accepting with resignation whatever befalls us. Jesus is talking about an active self-denial and a purposeful taking up of the cross. He is telling his disciples what would soon become obvious to them, that discipleship would be costly. They had decided to follow a leader who would be condemned to death as a criminal; and if they remained faithful to him, they would be painted with the same brush. The history of the early generations of the church, with its martyrs and persecutions, clearly bore this out. As Dietrich Bonhoeffer would say, and eventually proved in his own death, "when Christ calls, he bids one to come and die."

Taking Up the Cross Today

What are some concrete ways in which we are able to take up the cross in our daily lives? What are some actions and/or attitudes that should result from this taking up of the cross?

Taking Up the Cross Today

We today live in a different time and a different situation. While there are still countries where Christians are persecuted for their faith, most of us do not live in such circumstances. Most of us do not have to fear death for the mere fact of declaring ourselves followers of the Crucified. Even the cross has changed its symbolism, so that today it is no longer a sign of opprobrium or an instrument of torture. What, then, can be the meaning for us of this call of Jesus, to deny ourselves and take up the cross?

Notice first of all that taking up the cross is preceded by self-denial. Perhaps this is the more difficult part of this call from Jesus. It is not a matter of doing something heroic. It is a matter of doing something even more difficult: taking ourselves out of the center of things. At various times, Christians have attempted to deny themselves in extraordinary ways. Some have punished their bodies with flagellations and extreme fasting. Some have sat atop a pillar for years and years. Some have mutilated themselves. Some have vowed a life of celibacy to which they were not called. While there is something admirable in this sort of commitment, and while discipline is necessary in the Christian life, the problem with much of this sort of self-denial is that it still places oneself at the center of things, and therefore does not really deny oneself. It denies one's desires, or one's pleasures, or even one's needs; but it does not deny oneself in the radical sense of displacing the center of one's life. Actually, an extremely heroic and ostentatious discipleship may well be just one more way of placing oneself at the center of things.

At this point, it may be well to remember that the cross is a shameful thing. A self-denial that includes taking up the cross is not ostentatious and feels no need for the heroic or the exceptional. It is a self-denial that does not even expect to be recognized as such. It is a self-denial that becomes a way of life, even a routine, with no clashing of cymbals or blaring of trumpets.

The Gospel of Luke makes this very clear by adding the word *daily*: "If any want to become my followers, let them deny themselves and take up their cross daily and follow me" (Luke 9:23). Jesus is not calling his disciples to one great, heroic act of obedience—although such an act may well be required of them. His call is to a daily self-denial one could almost say, to a new routine in life, a daily routine of self-denial, or even of death in things large and small.

Lost and Found ■

Quickly review some of the parables of the lost and found mentioned in the session. Tell a story of something you thought you had lost, and how you felt upon finding it.

Lost and Found

This new routine, this daily taking up of the cross, is a losing of one's own life, but a losing that is gain. Jesus says it plainly in the passage we are studying: "For those who want to save their life will lose it, and those who lose their life for my sake will find it."

There is great joy in finding. Remember the parables of Jesus about the lost sheep (Luke 15:3-7), the lost coin (8-10), and the lost son (11-32). In all of these parables there is a common theme of joy in finding what was lost. The joy in heaven over our own being found is greater than the illustrations of joy in these stories. And the overwhelming feeling when we ourselves find our lives through self-denial and the cross is one of great joy—joy at having really found our lives. Therefore, when Jesus speaks of finding one's life, he is not just talking about being rewarded and going to heaven. He is talking about a profound, joyous experience of finding what was lost. Remember what we saw in our first session, that our very existence is the result of our being called by the Word of God—the Word that became incarnate in Christ. That is who we are meant to be: the ones whom he called into existence, the ones whom he named as his. Finding life is finding that profound and hidden reality that was lost.

From Death to Life

From Death to Life ■

Read John 3:1-8. What does "born from above" (NRSV) or "born again" (NIV) mean to you? How can one be "born again" in contemporary life? What new possibilities does this phrase suggest for your life?

Other Bible Passages

Here are some other Bible references that may help you and your group reflect on the relationship between joy and suffering, between life and death: Hebrews 12:2; Colossians 3:1-17 (especially verses 3 and 4).

Finding life is a theme that appears throughout the New Testament. In the Gospel of John, it is expressed in terms of being born again (John 3:3-7). To be born again implies dying to the old life. But it is also a promise and a beginning of new life. Have you ever thought that if you had another chance you would do things differently? In a way, that is precisely what being born again is all about. We celebrate the birth of a child because we recognize the myriad possibilities for this new life. When we are born again, there is celebration—even in heaven—because what was lost has been found. This dying and rising with Christ is a call to new possibilities, to joy, to victory.

Jesus calls us to deny ourselves, to take up the cross, and even to die to the old life. But

Concluding Prayer

End the session with a prayer:

Dear God, You know that we do not like for things to be difficult. Yet, we know that Easter follows after Good Friday, and that as we give up our own lives for your sake, we find them anew. We pray that you will let us know the joy of your salvation, the joy of finding our true life in you. Help us set aside our false securities and our vain hopes, and find in you our true security and our neverending hope. Help us to take up our cross today, and every day, and give us each day the joy of new life. In the name of Jesus, who is Life and Joy. Amen.

in our lives, as in the life of Jesus, the cross does not have the last word. The last word is one of victory and of joy!

Session Five

Jesus Calls Into Family

Session Focus ■
This session centers on the church as family of God. When Jesus calls us, he calls us into this family. In order to understand what this means, we will consider the meaning of the word *family*. We will also explore some of the connections between these issues and the present crisis of the family in most industrialized societies.

Session Objective ■
To have a deeper understanding of the root causes of the present crisis in the family. Also, to see how the church is a family, how this relates to its own calling from Jesus, and how it may help one respond to the difficulties now facing the family as an institution.

Session Preparation ■
Before the session, clip news items that point to the crisis of the family in our society. These may be reports about abandoned children, abused women, lonely elderly people, crime within a family, and so forth. They may also be statistics about rates of divorce, family violence,

(Matthew 12:46-50)

The Importance of Family

Family values are very important in our society, as they are in every human society. Indeed, one of the first things we learned in social studies in grade school was that the family is the basic building block of any society. Family is important, because no human being can subsist on its own. We all need structures of support, people who are sufficiently close to us to understand our deepest hopes and fears; people who carry us through difficult times when hope wavers. It is true that not everybody lives in a "family" in the common sense of the word. Many people live alone. Some have no close living relatives. Some are alienated from relatives. But even so, in order to be healthy everybody needs some sort of "family," in the sense of a close group of people who provide identity, support, relationship, and a sense of belonging. In the Bible, the people of God are sometimes called the "family"—or the "household"—of God. (See for instance 1 Peter 4:17.)

Thus, family has become a symbol for close community. That is why when we want to affirm that someone is close and dear to us, we say that she (or he) is "like family." When a family works at its best, it is the

Choose from among these activities and discussion starters to plan your lesson.

The Importance of Family ■

Look at the news clippings related to crisis in the family. What do the clippings say to you about the importance of the family?

Called Into Family ■

Read Genesis 1 and 2. Note God's use of the terms *good* and *not good*. What does the use of the terms in Genesis suggest to you about God's view of creation with regard to family?

place where people feel safe and free to be themselves, without pretenses or equivocations. For the same reason, dysfunctional families are a major tragedy that affects both the members of those families and, through them, the whole of society.

Called Into Family From the Time of Creation Itself

Being born into a family is part of the very order of creation. The Word who calls us into existence has made us in such a way that we need each other and the support of some sort of a family. A butterfly lays its eggs and then leaves them to fend for themselves. In contrast, human beings are born feeble and quite unable to survive on their own. They must be fed, and cleaned, and protected from all sorts of dangers. Otherwise, they will not survive. We have been created in such a way that even our physical survival itself depends on some sort of family.

What is true of our physical survival is also true of our emotional health and survival. Again, I remember how sad I was when I saw Bambi grow up into a stag and leave his family. Part of that sadness had to do with the pains of growing up. But part of it had to do with a deep difference between Bambi and me. Bambi was made in such a way that he would eventually roam the woods alone, looking for food and for a doe. I was made in such a way that I need a network of people around me. For me, as for every human being, such a network—some sort of "family"—is not just a matter of physical survival; it is also a matter of emotional survival, of full freedom to be myself, of personal identity.

The need to be in families, and families themselves, are a gift from God. Family is what theologians would call "an order of creation." In every society, no matter what its religion or its culture, there is a sense of family.

Families Don't Always Work

Yet, family life is not always pretty. In the Bible, almost at the very beginning of Genesis, Cain kills his brother Abel. This is a terrible crime. But what makes it particularly terrible is that it is a paradigm for what siblings have continued doing to each other through the ages. We do not need to go to Genesis to find such a barbaric violation of family. All we have to do is read the newspapers. In Genesis itself the story of the corruption of family continues. Abraham and Sarah abuse and evict Hagar and Ishmael. Jacob cheats Esau of his inheritance, and Esau seeks to kill him for that. Joseph's brothers sell him into slavery. It is a horrible story. And yet, once again, we do not need to go to Genesis to find such stories. Just look at the news: parents sell their children; husbands abuse and kill their wives; courts must intervene to settle disputes among siblings who gather around their parents' inheritance like vultures around a corpse.

While all of this has been true through the ages, it seems to have become worse in recent times, particularly in Western society. In the United States as well as in Europe, the divorce rate has soared to the point that a successful and lasting marriage seems to be the exception rather than the rule. In a society that appears to be growing increasingly violent, most violent crimes are committed within the family, against other family members.

As a result, there is a widespread and increasing call for "family values," hoping

Families Don't Always Work

What are some other examples of dysfunctional families in the Bible? Can you think of other examples in history? (Look, for instance, at the stories of fratricide among ruling families.)

that through legislation, communal pressure, moral teaching, or a combination of these, such values may be restored. There is much to be said for this effort. Certainly the rampant individualism of our modern culture, where the most important values are *my* freedom, *my* success, *my* happiness, undermines the family structure. This is not new. Jacob wanted to "get ahead," no matter what the cost; and with the connivance of his mother, he cheated his brother Esau out of his inheritance, which led to a long-lasting family feud. What is indeed new is that today there are many more complex and attractive ways to "get ahead" at the expense of others or by ignoring others and their claim on our lives.

On the other hand, if we do not understand the deeper roots of the modern crisis in the family, we will not be able to find adequate solutions. It is true that in Western society today, the family is in crisis as never before. But it was in crisis before we even knew it. Indeed, the crisis is so deep that even what we today would call a "good" family structure is itself the result of the crisis.

Put in a nutshell, the crisis began with the demise of the extended family. Throughout most of history, a "family" has been much more than a couple of parents and their children. In ancient times, families often included servants and their children as well as aunts and uncles, cousins, grandparents, grand uncles, and so on. A family was a vast network of people held together by various links, usually of kinship. When I was growing up in Cuba, if someone had asked me how many people were in my family, I would not have been able to tell. For one thing, they were too many to count—parents, brother, cousins, uncles, aunts, second cousins, and on, and on, and on. For another, I wouldn't know where to stop, for families did not have distinct limits, and one could always go a bit further. And, third, I belonged to more than one family. There were relatives on my mother's side, and on my father's side, and on my cousin's side by marriage, and so on.

One of the few places in which there still remains a vestige of the notion of "family" as the extended family is the "family reunion." Those who gather for such reunions usually have a common ancestor, but they now live quite apart from one another, sometimes at a great distance, and gather periodically to exchange news and rebuild connections.

With the Industrial Revolution, and particularly with the general mobility that began in the sixteenth century and became prevalent in the twentieth, such extended families became less and less common, and less and less functional. I have family whom I haven't seen for over 40 years. People move from one place to another seeking jobs, education, freedom, or whatever; and in so doing they leave behind the remainders of the extended family. It is for this reason that we have redefined the very word *family*, so that now it means what should more exactly be termed a "nuclear family": parents and their children, usually living under the same roof.

One should not romanticize the extended family. They, too, can be dysfunctional. In the extended families I knew in my youth, everyone had an uncle of whom one was ashamed, or a cousin, or a parent. Every family had members they knew could not be trusted. There were those who would only remember that they were family when they were in need. There was abuse of children and spouses, and sometimes also the elderly.

Family Reunions

Tell about a family reunion either in your family or in the family of someone you know. What does *family* mean in the context of a "family reunion"? How is it different from what has become the common understanding of "family"?

On the other hand, such extended families provided something that the present-day nuclear family cannot usually offer: an entire network of substitute role models whenever an expected role model failed. My parents were excellent parents—I cannot imagine any better. And yet, I did not have to count on my father as my only male role model. He was very good at human relations, at expressing ideas and feelings, at setting standards of conduct; but when it came to fixing things, when it came to sports, when it came to practical and detailed planning, I had to look to others for role models. And they were there, from an almost-uncle by marriage who was a well-known baseball pitcher to a distant cousin who could plan and fix anything. Something similar could be said about my mother and the other feminine role models I had around me.

By contrast, in a modern nuclear family the father is expected to be the male role model and the mother the female role model for all children in all spheres of life. That is patently impossible. It places on parents expectations that cannot be fulfilled. The situation is even more difficult in single-parent families. Indeed, for some parents the burden becomes so heavy that they simply opt out—thus contributing to the divorce and abandonment rates.

To all this, the late twentieth century has added another factor whose consequences we can barely foresee: the development of technology has been such, and so rapid, that many children who are not even teenagers know more than their parents in matters having to do with computers, cyberspace, and the like. Children growing up a few years ago were profoundly aware that their parents knew more than they did. Today, it is

New Generational Gaps ■

How often do you go to children, grandchildren, or other young persons in the family when faced with computer difficulties? How is this action different from our traditional way of learning? Do you think this undercuts the authority of an older generation to transmit social and moral values to the younger? Why so? Why not?

common for a child to experience its parent as a klutz who has difficulty installing a program in a computer, or finding certain information on the Internet. What this will mean for the future of parental authority remains to be seen; but it does not bode well for the future integrity of the nuclear family.

Thus, the present crisis in family life and family values needs to be understood at two levels. Viewed from the perspective of the many centuries of recorded history, the family has always been in crisis. Violence, infidelity, abuse, and oppression have always marred family life. But viewed from the perspective of the more recent crisis in Western societies, the present crisis has to do with the demise of the extended family as a result of the industrial revolution and modern mobility. Viewed from the first perspective, dysfunctional families are one more expression of the power of sin that has twisted and corrupted all of God's good creation. Viewed from the second perspective, the present crisis is due to the radical changes that have taken place in modern life. In either case, in order to respond to the crisis in the family it will not suffice to call for "family values," or to elect a particular party or a particular leader.

How Can the Church Respond?

Discuss: What is your church doing in response to the family crisis? (Or invite a report from the person whom you may have asked to do an interview.) What else could be done? What are other groups doing?

How Can the Church Respond?

Faced by the present crisis, churches have responded in a number of ways. Some churches have instituted programs to teach family values to the new generations. These certainly are necessary and valuable, for it is easy for upcoming generations, faced by a world that seems to be changing constantly, to think that the wisdom humankind has gleaned through the centuries is no longer valid. Yet, when all is said and done, it is clear that fidelity, trust and dependability, mutual support, loving intimacy, and other such values have proven their worth again and again—particularly in contrast with lives lived according to other values. When we teach such values, we are communicating the wisdom distilled from millennia of human history, of trial and error. It is important that we all—and particularly the younger generations—come to understand that even after the drastic changes of modern life ancient wisdom still stands, and that one forsakes its teachings at one's peril.

Many churches have instituted family support crisis intervention programs. These include pastoral counseling, marriage enrichment programs, family-oriented events, and the like. They also include shelters for abused women and children, homes for the homeless (for homelessness is also a family crisis) and many other such programs. These too are valuable and necessary, and at this point the churches are to be commended, for they have played a role in our society that is unequaled by any other institution, public or private.

Churches have also tried to intervene in the policy-making decision of government, both at the national and at various other levels. Thus, churches have lobbied for legislation providing support for needy families, for single mothers, for working parents needing child care, for those lacking medical services or medical insurance, for the elderly, and many other such programs. This also is a valid and important response to the crises in which many families find themselves in our society.

In our changing society, churches have also sought to redefine the family so as to include many people who are not part of "traditional" families. Increasing numbers of people today do not live in a "traditional" family, that is, in a nuclear family composed of parents and children, all under a single roof. Many live by themselves, either by choice or by necessity. Many children live with only one parent, or with a grandparent or another relative. Many are alienated from their birth families and live in other arrangements. This has led many churches to re-define what they mean by a "family," and to develop "family-oriented" programs that take into account the wide variety of conditions and arrangements in which people live today, so that, for instance, single-parent families will not feel excluded. That too is good, for loving inclusion is an important Christian value.

A Jarring Word From Jesus

A Jarring Word From Jesus ■

Read Matthew 12:46-50 and Matthew 10:34-39. What connections do you see in these two difficult passages? Does one of them help understand the other? If so, how?

In the midst of all this activity, and of all these efforts by churches to strengthen family life, Matthew 12:46-50 sounds a jarringly discordant note. In this story, the one who tells him that his family is outside seems to take for granted that Jesus will be in favor of "family values." Certainly, even though he is teaching the crowds, when he hears that his mother and his brothers are standing outside waiting to talk with him, he will take a break, tell the crowd to wait, and go speak with his kin. Jesus, however, is not ready to take a break. Rather, he uses the very presence of his mother and brothers to further his teaching of the crowds, telling them that his disciples, those who do the will of his Father in heaven, are his kin, which is also indirectly inviting all who hear him to become part of his family.

The discordant note is so strong that in shock we often exaggerate it. Jesus does not say that Mary is no longer his mother, or that his brothers are no longer his brothers. He simply expands the definition of kindred in an unexpected way, so that now he has many more mothers, sisters, and brothers: "For whoever does the will of my Father in heaven is my brother and sister and mother."

Still, the story does not seem particularly supportive of family values. And it is made even more jarring if we remember that this is not the only saying of Jesus where he sounds a similar note. On occasion, he even declares that "whoever comes to me and does not hate father and mother, wife and children, brothers and sisters, yes, and even life itself, cannot be my disciple" (Luke 14:26). These are harsh words, even if the original Greek word is not as strong as the English word *hate*. Wasn't Christianity supposed to strengthen the family? Weren't we told that "the family that prays together stays together"?

I must confess that I probably find these passages less jarring than many of my readers, for as I was growing up as a Protestant in a mostly Roman Catholic country, I had friends in church who had been disinherited by their parents and expelled from their homes because they had decided to join the church. One friend, a student from another country, had been met at the door by his father wielding a shotgun and telling him never to come back. Another had been ditched by her fiancé two months before their wedding, because she insisted on going to church. While the conflict between Protestants and Catholics has abated, for other reasons many people, even in today's world, are confronted with the difficult choice between giving up their family and giving up their faith.

God's Family

How do you think Jesus' definition of *family* as those who "do the will of God" can contribute to the strengthening of family values in contemporary culture? What might happen in our daily lives if we lived according to his vision of family?

God's Family

Still, the words of Jesus come to us as a shock. They come as a shock, because Jesus redefines the meaning of *family*. He proposes a new family—one that does not necessarily undo the bonds of the previous families, but certainly one that is not limited by those bonds. There is a new family. This is the family of those who do the will of the heavenly Parent. It is the family of the children of God. It is not the Jones family, or the Smith or the Pérez family. It is the family of God— or, as First Peter would say, "the household of God" (4:17).

While our initial reaction to these words is understandable, it is also true that they make perfect sense if we really believe what Jesus teaches and promises. Christian faith is about a new birth. If family is a matter of birth and parentage, we should not be surprised that the new birth results also in a new family: the "household of God," those who do the will of Jesus' Father.

Remember what you studied earlier in Session One, that in a sense all Christians have the same last name: *Godschild*, or if you wish, *Christian*. We are not baptized into separate families, but into the family of God. Remember the connection between calling as summoning and calling as naming. In summoning us, Jesus also gives us, so to speak, a new family name. In this extended family that is the church, we are John Christian, Nkwame Christian, and Suk Yoon Christian. The same is true of an adult being baptized, who now joins a new family of faith.

This is one reason why, when baptizing a child, the pastor takes the child in her or his arms. Although sometimes the meaning of this act is lost in sentimentalism, it actually symbolizes that, in a sense, the parents present a child and are given back a brother or a sister. In baptism, even though we seldom say it, the parents symbolically relinquish any claim to absolute authority over their children.

The Church as a New Extended Family ■

List some ways your church can strengthen its role as an "extended family." What can you as an individual member of your "church family" do to strengthen its role as an extended family?

The Church as a New Extended Family

One of the difficulties we have speaking of the church as a family is that too often when we hear that phrase we think in terms of a nuclear family. By definition, a nuclear family is a limited number of people, not open to others who may wish to join. Its limits are precise: some belong to it, and some simply don't—and that can never change. In contrast, an extended family is open. Its limits are imprecise. It does not preclude belonging to other families. On the contrary, it requires it, for it is the network of all these various extended families that provides the fabric for society. A healthy extended family is always open to others; and others come to it by various means, not along a single, prescribed route.

It is to such a family that Christ calls us. The One who made us in such a way that we need families in order to survive and to grow has also created a new family for those who heed the call and follow the way of discipleship. Just as in the order of creation it is impossible to survive without a family, without others who support us and care for us, so in the order of redemption it is impossible to survive and to grow as a disciple without this family of mothers, sisters, and brothers of Jesus as well as ours. When Jesus called us into existence, he called us into a family. Now, as he calls us into discipleship, he calls us into the family of all disciples, the church.

This is particularly significant in our modern age, when the nuclear family is in crisis

Closing Worship

Hold hands with one another. Read or sing the hymn "In Christ There Is No East or West." Imagine Christians in faraway places, from other cultures and races. Think about what it means that they too are part of the same family. Conclude with the following prayer:

Oh God, you who are the Parent of us all, teach us how to live as a loving family. We know that in calling us to follow Christ you have also called us to be his sisters and brothers, and also brothers and sisters of each other. Remind us of this whenever we fail to see our kinship, whenever differences of culture, gender, class, race, or anything else would divide us and set us one against the other. We know that it is only in the community of your household that we can be faithful to our calling. Give us the wisdom, the power, and the grace to be your loving family. In the name of Jesus, our brother who has called us to you and to each other. Amen.

and the old extended families can no longer be reconstructed. One could even say that the church is called to be the new extended family that God is offering to all of us, children of an age that by leaving aside the values of the extended family finds itself in a crisis where the nuclear family is hardly sustainable. This is clearly the experience of many immigrants, who feel the pain of being uprooted from the extended families that shaped and supported them, and now find a new family in the church. This is why in many immigrant churches one usually speaks of "the church family," rather than of "the families of the church."

It is clear that in this extended family that is the church there are still problems. Sin has not disappeared. Unfortunately, in the church too there is dysfunction, disloyalty, self-seeking, and sometimes even violence. But, just as in the case of our birth families, it is to this family we belong. It is in it that we are called to grow. It is the church that we are called to shape and love and reform, so that it may be more like what it is intended to be, what it will be in the final day. The church, imperfect as it is, is a support system God has provided for all of us who heed the call and who, as babes in the faith, need a family of faith to nurture us as we grow and to support us as we face life's crises as well as the many unexpected dimensions of our call.

Session Six

Jesus Calls Into Service

Session Focus ■

In this session we shall center our attention on the service of others as a call from Jesus. We shall see that Jesus calls us and meets us in the needy. We will also deal with some of the excuses that are sometimes offered for not serving those in need.

Session Objective ■

To become aware that there is no conflict or tension between the religious service of God and the service of God to the needy and to understand that service to others is an act of worship.

Session Preparation ■

If you have access to books on Christian art, you may find some pictures representing Martin of Tours sharing his cape with the beggar. This is a fairly common theme in Christian art, and the most common way to represent Martin. There are several such paintings and representations on the Internet, which you can copy and print. Look, for instance, at the Web site: *http://www.catholicforum.com/saints/saintm07.htm*

(Matthew 25:31-46)

Where Do We Find Jesus?

It is clear that the essence of the call of Jesus is to follow him. But, where do we find him, now that he is no longer physically with us? There are several answers to this question. Obviously, we find Jesus in the Gospels and in the whole of Scripture. It is there that we learn of his teachings, his life, his ministry, and of God's plans for creation and for us. That is why we do studies such as this, searching in Scripture for the meaning and content of our call. We also find him, as we have just seen in our last session, in the community of the faithful, the household of God. Throughout the centuries, Christians have been particularly aware that we meet him in the midst of that community at the Lord's Supper, and therefore, this has been an important aspect of worship—and also, unfortunately, a bitter subject for debate among believers of different denominations. Worship, preaching, and the sacraments are places where we hear the call of Jesus. It is also true that we find him and hear him in private prayer, Scripture reading, and meditation, when we open ourselves to his lordship and guidance.

The Presence of Jesus in the Needy

Choose from among these activities and discussion starters to plan your lesson.

Where Do We Find Jesus? ■

Form teams of two or three. Talk about the places where you "find Jesus." Where and how do you sense the presence of Jesus Christ?

The Presence of Jesus in the Needy ■

Read Matthew 25:31-46. What challenges you in this Scripture? What opportunities do you see for experiencing the presence of Jesus Christ?

There is, however, one other place where we meet Jesus, and which merits special attention. Jesus himself has told us that he comes to us in the needy. Look at the passage we are studying today. We can read it as a commandment to feed the hungry, cover the naked, and visit the sick. But it is more than that. It is also a promise that Jesus will come to us in those who need our service and support. He does not say that he was watching as we fed the hungry—or as we did not. He does not say that we gave good witness to him as we clothed the naked—or that we gave a negative testimony if we did not clothe them. Clearly, these things are true. But he says much more than that. He says that he actually was hungry *in* the hungry, naked *in* the naked, thirsty *in* the thirsty.

These are strange words indeed. Jesus tells us that he will be coming to us even while we await his final coming to judge the nations. But he will not come as a powerful ruler, as a rich bestower of gifts, or as an admired religious teacher. He will come as a hungry woman, a naked child, a lonely old man. In a way, this is consistent with his first coming to us, when he was not born in a palace in a great capital city but in a stable in the little town of Bethlehem. It is also consistent with what he told his disciples, that in the nations around us the powerful lord it over the weak; but among his disciples the great will be those who serve. And it certainly is consistent with his claim to victory through suffering and the cross, and with his call to his disciples to follow the same path. The disciples of the Crucified will find him, not as a senator in imperial Rome or as a respected philosopher in wise Athens, but

Martin of Tours ■

Read the entire story in the *Life of Saint Martin,* by Sulpitius Severus, chapter 3. Various translations of it are readily available. Or enter *Martin of Tours* into a search program like *www.google.com* or *www.yahoo.com.* Prepare a brief presentation based on your research.

as a beggar in the streets, as a convict in the mines, as a child reaching out for food.

There is an old story about a newly converted Christian in the fourth century. His name was Martin, and he was originally from distant Pannonia, in what today is Hungary. Martin, who was then a 20-year-old soldier, had not even been baptized when, in the city of Amiens in France, he saw a beggar shivering in the cold at the city gates. Being a poor soldier, Martin had no money to give him. But he had his soldier's cape, which he rent in two and then gave half to the beggar. While this put to shame some who could have helped the beggar with much less sacrifice, it also drew the scorn of those who passed by and saw him half naked. Finally, in spite of the cold, he was able to sleep. In the middle of the night he had a dream in which he saw Christ coming to him, dressed in half a soldier's cape, and he heard Jesus saying to the multitude of angels surrounding him: "Martin, who is not even baptized yet, had clothed me with his cape." At this point, Martin's biographer comments that Jesus was fulfilling his promise, "Inasmuch as you did it to one of these . . . you did it to me."

Our words *chapel* and *chaplain* are connected with the story of Martin. In the Middle Ages, what was purported to be a piece of Martin's cape was very highly regarded and closely guarded. This "little cape" or *capella,* was kept in a small church that eventually was also called *capella;* and a person entrusted with guarding it was a *capellanus.* Hence "chapel" and "chaplain."

Martin's dream may well have been no more than that; but in any case it points to an important truth: When Martin was sharing his cape with the beggar, he and the beggar were not alone. There was a Third One with them. The One who had said 300 years earlier, "Inasmuch as you did it . . ." was there, coming to Martin through the person of the beggar.

Likewise, when Mother Teresa of Calcutta was asked how she could work so constantly in the service of the poor, quite often working in circumstances that would otherwise seem physically disgusting and repelling, she explained that she knew that in serving the poor and the ill in Calcutta she was serving Jesus. Those whom others saw as dirty and repulsive, she saw as stand-ins for Jesus. For Mother Teresa, this was a way in which she served and worshiped her Master.

The Sacrament of Service

It is so in every act of Christian service. Christ is really present in those whom we serve. So much so, that some have spoken of "the sacrament of service." Just as the Lord comes to us in baptism and the Lord's Supper, so does he come to us in the needy. Unfortunately, sometimes Christians have argued among themselves about which is more important, worship or service. The truth is that the two cannot be contrasted so starkly. Perhaps that is why we often speak of a "worship service." At any rate, we should certainly speak of our service to others as an act of worship to the One who calls us to serve.

Since in this study we are speaking in terms of call, one could say that in the needy Jesus is saying, "Come to me, and serve me, for I am hungry, and I am thirsty, and I am naked, and I am in prison." Jesus calls us, not only through Scripture, and worship, and study, and prayer but also in every person in need whom we meet.

Mother Teresa ▓

Enter the words *Mother Teresa* in a search program like *www.google.com* or *www.yahoo.com*. Read about Mother Teresa of Calcutta in the resources listed. Prepare a brief report for the group.

The Sacrament of Service ▓

What connections do you make between "worship" and "service"? How can service be worship? What similarities do you see? What differences?

Worship of God and Service to Others

To illustrate the connection between these two, you may relate the story of "The Theologian's Tale: The Legend Beautiful," a poem by Henry Wadsworth Longfellow in Tales of a Wayside Inn. *In the poem, Longfellow tells of a monk who had a vision of Jesus just as the convent bell summoned him to feed the poor. After much debate, the monk decided to go do his duty, even though it meant painfully leaving the Vision behind. After performing his duty, the monk returned to his cell, and Longfellow told us:*

"But he paused with awe-struck feeling
At the threshold of his door,
For the Vision was still standing
As he left it there before,
When the convent bell appalling,
From its belfry calling, calling,
Summoned him to feed the poor.
Through the long hour intervening
It has waited his return,
And he felt his bosom burn,
Comprehending all the meaning,
When the Blessed Vision said,
'Hadst thou stayed, I must have fled!' "

All Are Needy

List some of the needs you see in your daily life. List such things as basic needs (shelter, food, and so forth) and inner needs (love, understanding, company, purpose in life, and so forth). Read the list and consider whether any of the needs apply to you or to people close to you. How might this awareness of your needs limit your

All Are Needy

If this is true, one can also say that Jesus calls us from every person whom we meet, for there is not a single person in this world who is not in need of something. Some are in need of material things such as food, water, shelter, and clothing. Others are in need of company, love, understanding, and encouragement. All are in need of God. If one thing binds all humankind together, it is that we are all in need. The situation is not desire to help others? expand your desire to help others? help you to experience Jesus Christ present within you and within others?

simply one in which some only give and some only receive. On the contrary, in every giving we also receive, and in every receiving we also give.

This means, among other things, that the call to us from the needy is a two-way call. We see somebody in need, and in serving that person we are serving Jesus himself. But there is always a sense in which we too are needy, and that other person fills our need. It could be, for instance, that we need to have a sense of purpose in our lives. In that case, we may find that sense of purpose in teaching the illiterate how to read. The illiterate are to us a call from Jesus, who some day will say to us, "I was illiterate, and you taught me how to read." We may also come to that illiterate person as people in need of purpose, and in that case someday Jesus will say to that illiterate person, "I was looking for a purpose in life, and you gave it to me."

It is important to recognize this. If we do not, we shall feel guilty in our very acts of service, which always have a tinge or at least a possibility of paternalism or patronizing; and such guilt may well paralyze us. Indeed, one of the most common excuses for not serving the needy is that in so doing we would be simply filling our need to feel useful, important, and needed. We tell ourselves that, since such feelings lead to a patronizing attitude, we should not serve the needy. Thus, in claiming to avoid paternalistic attitudes, we also avoid our responsibility toward those in need. But, why not acknowledge our own need? Why not acknowledge that we need to feel needed, and that we find this need met in serving others? Obviously it is not good to be patronizing or paternalistic. However, the best way to avoid this is not by avoiding the needy but rather by serving them and at the same time acknowledging, both to ourselves and to others, that the openly needy, whom we serve, are also meeting our own needs.

Look at it another way. You are following this study because you feel a need to come closer to Jesus and to his will for you, to come closer to your calling. If Jesus himself were to come to you right now and ask you to do something, that would be meeting your need—as it certainly would be meeting mine! Would you say, "Now Lord, I really would like to respond to you, but since that would be meeting my own need for you, I'd better not"? Can you imagine Peter by the sea of Galilee saying, "Lord, I really would like to follow you; but since that would be meeting my needs, I had better stay with my boats"?

That is precisely what happens when we see someone in need. Jesus is calling us, just as clearly and as personally as when he called Peter: "I am hungry. I am in prison. I am lonely." There is no doubt that this call meets some of your deepest needs. That is what the call of Jesus is all about!

A Network of Giving and Receiving ■

Read I Corinthians 12:12-26. In the body, which members receive? which give? What does the Scripture say to you about the network of giving and receiving in daily life?

A Network of Giving and Receiving

Serving and being served, giving and receiving, thus become no longer a means to claim superiority or to patronize the other but a two-way relationship in which all are blessed. Furthermore, what we receive is then passed on to others, just as what we give moves on.

Paul illustrates the serving and being served with the image of the body in 1 Corinthians 12:12-26. Obviously, all the parts of the body give and receive. The eye cannot despise the foot, because it receives transportation from the foot; but at the same time, the foot receives vision through the eye. Without the foot, the eye could not go from place to place. Without the eye, the foot would not know where to go.

In Session Five we spoke of the family. In a way, a family is a network of giving and receiving. Parents provide nurture, care, and guidance to children; but children also meet many of their parents needs. In a healthy family, people help each other without even thinking about it. They do not stop to think how many favors they have done for another or how many they are owed in return. They simply give, because that is the nature of the relationship. Actually, a healthy family would be surprised if someone were to describe it as a network of giving and receiving—and yet, that is precisely what it is. Likewise, even though in a sense we know that in serving others we are serving Christ, in another sense we are surprised by that very fact.

At a friend's funeral a few days ago, the pastor read some words that my friend had written to the effect that we can only give because we have received, and that those who give to us have in turn received from others. He went on to compare this passing on of gifts to apostolic succession. As I sat listening to these words, it occurred to me that there is a sort of apostolic succession to giving and receiving. Over the centuries, various groups of Christians have convinced themselves that they are the true church of Christ, because they can claim an uninterrupted line of succession for their leaders. While such claims and debates over apostolic succession have divided the church, what has always united it is the network of giving and receiving that perhaps could be called "service succession." What we have, we have received from others—even from others completely unknown to us. What we give will pass on through generations to others whose existence we can hardly dream of. Thus the church is a network of love, tied together by bonds of giving and receiving, by service to each other, and by service to the world.

Service, like love, is never used up. It is not spent when given. On the contrary, it grows and multiplies: it comes back to the one rendering the service, and it also moves on to others along the long line of "service succession," so that its effects reach far and wide.

What ideas or insights about Christian life and the call of Jesus Christ do the words *service succession* suggest to you?

They Did Not Know

There is another side to this text. The way Jesus told the story, those who served him were not aware that they were doing so, and those who did not were not aware that they were refusing Jesus himself. Both groups were surprised: "Lord, when did we see you . . . ?"

In a way, this means that we stand at a different place than those about whom the story is told. They were surprised. They did not know. Those who did not serve their neighbors in need could at least claim ignorance, even though, according to the text, such a claim would not avail for them. But we cannot even claim ignorance. We have been told. We have the clear words of Jesus: "Just as you did [or did not do] it to one of these . . . you did [or did not do] it to me." Precisely because we have read or heard the words of Jesus, we cannot claim to be caught unawares.

It is interesting and tragic to note that Christians have spent so much time discussing what beliefs are necessary for salvation, and that at times such discussions have drawn us away from service to the neighbor.

They Did Not Know ■

What surprises have you experienced as you served others? How do you think the habits of serving and loving might make a difference in your family? in your church? in your community? in the world? in your relationship with Jesus Christ?

We seem to think that Jesus will judge us according to our orthodoxy; and thus there are Christians who claim that if you do not believe this or that doctrine, you cannot be saved. Orthodoxy is important. What we believe does make a difference. But we must not forget this passage that points in a different direction. Here, people are judged not on the basis of what they believe but on the basis of their service to those in need.

This is not to say that orthodox Christian belief and service are opposites. On the contrary, if we believe in Jesus, and are convinced that his words are true, then we know that we must serve those in need, precisely because he says so. Those who truly believe Jesus will not be surprised, as are the people in the text we are studying, because we have been told in this very text. We know that in serving the needy we are serving Jesus. And we should also know that in neglecting and rejecting the needy we are neglecting and rejecting Jesus.

On the other hand, there is another sense in which there is a place for surprise. As Christians serve others, God uses those experiences to change our hearts, to make us more willing to serve, to create what could well be called the "habit" of service. Our walk with Christ, our hearing his call to discipleship, to take up the cross, to rejoice in newness of life, all of that also creates in us a new heart and a new spirit. The more we serve others, the more it becomes second nature for us. It is a common experience that the more we give, the easier giving becomes. The more we love, the easier loving becomes. Likewise, as service becomes part of our new life in Christ, the point comes when we serve others, not because Christ commands us to do so, or even because in that other person we see Christ himself, but because Christ, living in us, impels us to do so.

At this point, Christian service to those in need becomes an automatic response to need, something we do because that is who we are. And in this sense it does come to us as a surprise—as an almost daily surprise, and also as a surprise in the Final Judgment—that we have been serving Jesus.

Close With Worship ■

Either sing or read aloud the hymn, "Where Cross the Crowded Ways of Life," or the hymn, "O Master, Let Me Walk with Thee." Close with a few moments of silent prayer followed by the Lord's Prayer.

Session Seven

Jesus Calls Through Others

Session Focus ■

This session will focus on what Peter and the church learned from Cornelius rather than the other way around. However, it is clear that they did not learn these things from Cornelius himself but rather from the Lord, who used Cornelius to call both Peter and the church to greater obedience and a wider mission.

Session Objective ■

To be ready to hear the call of Jesus even in people from whom we should not expect such a call. We should be open to the possibility that Jesus may be teaching us something important through people who are not leaders in the church but outsiders just coming in. (This would include Christians in what we used to call the "mission field.")

Session Preparation ■

Have a map on the wall or in another visible place, showing the location of Caesarea and Joppa. Read in a Bible dictionary about both Caesarea and Joppa. In particular, note

(Acts 10)

Two Visions and Two Calls

In Acts, and throughout the history of the church, we see how Jesus continues calling people, even when he is not physically present. Jesus called Saul of Tarsus on the road to Damascus. Jesus called Timothy, and Priscilla, and Aquila, and the Ethiopian eunuch, and thousands of others.

The passage we are studying today, Acts 10, is usually called "the conversion of Cornelius." But it could just as well be called "the conversion of Peter," as we shall see in the course of our study. Indeed, if Jesus called Cornelius to discipleship through Peter, he also called Peter to new dimensions of discipleship through Cornelius.

At the heart of the story there are two visions, for both Peter and Cornelius had visions; and the two eventually came together. If we did not know the story and were told that both the apostle Peter and the Roman centurion Cornelius had visions, we would certainly expect Peter's vision to be the clearest and Cornelius's to be rather dim. After all, Peter had been with Jesus for several years, and he was now a preacher of the gospel, while Cornelius was a Gentile soldier in the army that had crucified Jesus, an army of pagans who worshiped an array of that Caesarea, even though built fairly close to Jerusalem, was essentially a Gentile city. Look up the word *God-fearer* in a Bible dictionary. Or read a commentary on Acts where the meaning of being a "God-fearer" or a "devout person" is clarified.

Choose from among these activities and discussion starters to plan your lesson.

Two Visions and Two Calls ■

Form two teams. One will represent Peter, and the other Cornelius. Now follow through the narrative in Acts with several stops in chronological order: *First stop*—Before any of the visions. What has Peter been doing? Read Acts 9:36-43. How do you think he must have felt? assured? confused? What was Cornelius doing? Read Acts 10:1-2. How do you think he must have felt? assured? confused? undecided? *Second stop.* Read Acts 10:3-8. What has changed? *Third stop.* Read Acts 10:9-17. What has changed now? Is Peter as assured as he was before? Is he confused? *Fourth stop.* Read Acts 10:25-33. What feelings or thoughts occur to you now? What have you learned? *Final stop.* Read Acts 10:34-36, 44-48. What about now? What has changed?

gods and even the emperor. But that is not what happened.

As we compare the two visions, we are struck by the contrast between Peter's vision, which is somewhat blurred and confusing, and Cornelius's, which is clear and detailed. Read the text. Peter saw an undefined "something like a white sheet." He heard a voice telling him three times to kill and eat what was on the sheet, and three times he refused. At the end, "the thing" was taken back to heaven, and the result was that Peter was "greatly puzzled." In contrast, Cornelius had a vision in which he "clearly" saw an angel. This angel gave clear instructions: "Now send men to Joppa for a certain Simon who is called Peter; he is lodging with Simon, a tanner, whose house is by the seaside." The only thing that could have made his instructions clearer would have been a zip code!

Another Reluctant Prophet

It is interesting to note that Peter was at Joppa when he received this apparently unwelcome call to go to the Gentiles. Joppa was the city where Jonah took a ship bound for Tarshish in order to avoid a similar call from God to go to the Gentiles. Jonah refused; Peter agreed. It is also interesting to note that Peter's actual name was "Simon, son of Jonah."

The contrast not only is in the matter of clarity but also in the matter of time. Cornelius had his vision long before Peter had his. Indeed, Peter's vision came only the next day, when the messengers sent by Cornelius were about to arrive at the house where Peter was lodging. As a postscript to his vision, which he still did not understand, Peter was told by the Spirit that he was to go with them and do as they requested.

Thus the two visions, one clear and the other somewhat puzzling, came to these two people in different places—in different places geographically (one is in Caesarea and the other in Joppa) and religiously (one is a Christian apostle and the other a pagan who has felt the impact of Judaism).

In Acts 10:2, Cornelius was called a "devout man who feared God." This placed him among the "godfearers." This was the name given in Judaism to those pagans who were attracted by the moral laws and the monotheism of Judaism, but who were not ready to follow the process of conversion into Judaism or to be circumcised and obey all the ritual laws of Israel.

Yet, in spite of the religious, cultural, and geographical distances between Peter and Cornelius, their visions and their callings converged. Until he had his vision, Cornelius did not even know that God had been preparing a man called Peter to come to him. And Peter was unaware of it even after he had the vision that prepared him for responding to Cornelius's request.

This is an important point to consider, for too often we think of the call of Jesus in individual terms. At best, we realize that our calling has come to us through the church, and that part of that calling is an invitation to join the community of believers. But our calling has connections and implications that reach much farther than we imagine. Right now, Jesus is calling others—some probably across the street and some halfway around the world. All of these calls, as well as yours and mine, have a personal dimension to them. They are also part of a great web of callings through which the Lord is bringing creation to its goal and fulfillment. I am convinced that writing these lines is part of my calling; yet I have no idea how the Lord will use them. Right now the Lord may be calling you to do something that has implications you and I cannot even suspect.

Peter's Conversion

Peter's Conversion ■

Are you now doing, thinking, and saying things that you would not have expected a few years ago? Are you sometimes surprised when you think about how much you have changed, how your vision has widened? Do you think that, as in the case of Peter, this may be the work of the Spirit? How? Why?

We often hear the story of the conversion of Cornelius and those gathered in his house; it needs little clarification. But look at the text again and consider what happened to Peter and his ideas and attitudes. He agreed to the request of Cornelius's envoys to go with them, because the Spirit had told him to do so. When he arrived at Cornelius's house, he reminded his host and all that were gathered that his presence there was a concession to the will of God, and it was nothing that he would likely do on his own. He said: "You yourselves know that it is unlawful for a Jew to associate with or to visit a Gentile; but God has shown me that I should not call anyone profane or unclean." In other words, if it were up to me, that is precisely what I would call you! I am here much against my will and my better inclinations; but God has commanded, and I obey.

At last, Peter began to understand his puzzling vision and to see its connection with the request that came from Cornelius. Much to his credit, Peter was obedient, even though he apparently did not like what he was told to do. Peter ended up doing precisely what a few days earlier he would not even have considered. (Sometimes I wonder if the reason why Peter was only given a puzzling vision was that, had he been told what he would be asked to do and some of its consequences, he would have balked.)

The story continues. Cornelius explained his vision to Peter, who responded by a theological statement he probably would not have made otherwise: "I truly understand that God shows no partiality, but in every nation anyone who fears him and does what is right is acceptable to him." From that point on, he launched into the story of Jesus in what appears to be his standard sermon, for it is similar to what he said at Pentecost.

In the middle of his speech, however, God surprised him once more. Acts tells us that the Holy Spirit fell on those who were listening so that they began speaking in tongues and glorifying God. Suddenly, Peter seems to have lost the initiative and control over the situation. He was telling them about God. Now it is they who extol God. Peter could have responded in outrage. They had invited him to speak, and now they apparently were no longer listening! But he responded with the openness that comes only from the unforseen action of the Spirit. He concluded that if the Holy Spirit had decided to come upon these people, it was not up to him to bar them from full communion in the church. And so he orders that they be baptized.

Then, at the end of the chapter, almost in passing, we receive a glimpse of the profound change that has taken place in Peter. This observant Jew, who considered it unlawful or at least extraordinary even to associate or to visit in the house of a Gentile, stayed with Cornelius and his friends for several days!

This is why one can say that this passage is not only about the conversion of Cornelius but also about the conversion of Peter. Cornelius, the pagan "devout man who feared God," became a Christian. And Peter converted from a narrow gospel limited to a particular people to a worldwide gospel open to people of all nations and races. Cornelius discovered what it means to be a Christian. Peter discovered something new about what it means to be a disciple.

The Conversion of the Church ■

Write on a chalkboard or large piece of paper: "Throughout the centuries, and already in Acts, the history of the church has been a history not only of growth and expansion but also of conversion." Read the statement aloud. Is this true? Can you mention moments or ways in which the church has been converted? (Think of the attitudes in the church toward slavery, for example.) Do you think that God is calling our church today to a new conversion? If so, how? What might be different?

The Conversion of the Church

If you continue reading the story as it develops in Acts 11, you will find that the church in Jerusalem was not happy with what Peter had done. Indeed, upon his return to Jerusalem they asked him: "Why did you go to uncircumcised men and eat with them?" (Acts 11:3). Apparently, Peter's original dislike for his mission to Cornelius was shared by the rest of the early Christian community, and they now called him to account.

Peter's response was simply to relate all that had happened (including both his vision and Cornelius's) leading to their receiving the Spirit. He concluded his narrative with his reason for doing what he did: "If then God gave them the same gift that he gave us when we believed in the Lord Jesus Christ, who was I that I could hinder God?" (Acts 11:17).

At this, the response of the believers in Jerusalem was one of amazed discovery: "Then God has given even to the Gentiles the repentance that leads to life" (Acts 11:18).

As we now look back through the centuries, this is probably the most important discovery that the church has ever made. It was such a radical departure from their earlier views that one can only speak of it as a conversion. The nascent church, until then limited to people of Abrahamic descent (with the possible exception of the Ethiopian eunuch, if the narrative in Acts follows a strict chronological order), now discovers that its message is for the entire world. Had it not been for that discovery, Christianity would have remained just one more of the many Jewish sects that have appeared through the ages, and its adherents would at best be a few thousand. But because of that discovery it was now possible and even necessary to preach the gospel throughout the world. This idea certainly was not new, for it was precisely what Jesus had told his disciples to do, as we shall see in our next session. But apparently the early disciples, through a combination of their early success among Jews in Jerusalem and their deeply rooted prejudices against Gentiles, had not remembered that commandment of Jesus and were quite content with remaining a movement within the Jewish community.

Had it not been for that discovery stated so briefly in Acts 11:18, I would not be a Christian today, nor would most of you who read this book. Indeed, most of us are not physical descendants of Abraham and Jacob and are therefore among those Gentiles to whom Peter would rather not go.

On the other hand, because of that momentous discovery Christianity soon spread throughout the Roman Empire and beyond, into Armenia, Persia, Ethiopia, India, and even China. Eventually, it would reach every corner of the earth, to the point that today it is the largest and the fastest-growing religion in the world—even though from our limited perspective it would sometimes not seem to be so.

New Forms of Obedience ■

What does the phrase "new forms of obedience" suggest

New Forms of Obedience

As one looks at this entire succession of events, one notices a strange series of calls. First of all, there is the call to Peter through to you? What do you think a new form of obedience would look like in your daily life? How does Acts 10 inform your vision of a "new form of obedience"?

Cornelius. We usually think that it is Christians who are to go out and call others to follow. That is usually the case, but this story reminds us of other possibilities. Here, Jesus calls Peter to do something and to learn something through the outsider Cornelius. We tend to think that we "take Christ" with us to new places. Here, however, we see that the Lord is already in those places, not only preparing the way for us but even using those new places and people as a way to call us to new forms of obedience.

Then there is the call to the church in Jerusalem. They considered themselves—with good reason—guardians of the truth, and they were concerned when they discovered that Peter had apparently been going beyond the bounds of accepted practice. Yet the Lord used Peter, and Peter's own experience of having learned from the work of the Spirit in Cornelius, to call the entire church to new forms of obedience.

Peter could do this because he had heeded the call of the Lord in Cornelius. The church now heeded the call of the Lord through Peter, and because of that heeding widened its mission to include Gentiles, and eventually even us!

I can imagine all sorts of reasons why Peter could have refused to heed the call through Cornelius. It just wasn't done! What would people think? He was not authorized to go to a pagan centurion in Caesarea.

I can also imagine all sorts of reasons why the church in Jerusalem would be inclined to disown what Peter had done. The church was already in trouble enough with the Jewish authorities, and this could well be the straw that broke the camel's back. What would the good religious people in Jerusalem say? Perhaps it would be best to develop a coherent strategy, seeking to convert all of Israel first, and then go to the Gentiles. Peter's successful mission to Cornelius eventually resulted in the church becoming mostly a Gentile institution. By its very success, the early Christian Jewish community lost control of the church. Yet Peter and eventually also the church in Jerusalem were led by the Spirit to overcome all these objections and to do something radically new.

Heirs to the Call

Heirs to the Call ■

What thoughts or feelings do you have about former "mission fields" in other parts of the world sending missionaries back to the Northern Hemisphere? What connections do you make between social issues in our contemporary culture and the "new form of obedience" suggested by Acts 10? Can you think of other situations in which God may be calling your own local congregation, or the entire denomination, into new paths of obedience?

We are all heirs to this strange sequence of callings. We are its heirs in the sense that we are its result. Without that sequence of callings most of us Gentile Christians would not have heard the preaching of the gospel. In many ways, the missionary enterprise of the nineteenth and twentieth century succeeded so that today the majority of Christians are in what we used to call "the mission field." But we are also heirs in the sense that we are presented similar challenges to which we can raise similar objections. Let us see a couple of examples.

First of all, one of the most astonishing developments of the twentieth century was that the numeric center of Christianity moved away from the Northern Hemisphere and is now in the South, in the countries usually called "the Third World." For generations, these churches were nurtured by us. From us they received the gospel, and from us they learned much of its meaning. Now, early in the twenty-first century, they have become strong churches. Many of them are growing rapidly, sending missionaries and teachers all over the world, and developing and sustaining their own institutions. In some cases, they are sending missionaries back to the Northern Hemisphere, to the same countries from which they first received the gospel.

It is easy for us to resist and even resent this. After all, they learned the gospel from us! We are the ones who sent them missionaries. Now they claim to have something to teach us. How can that be?

Or take another example. There are changes taking place in the society all around us. One such change has to do with justice in gender relations. The unequal relationships that were considered normative a century ago are now seen to be unjust. Women claim the right to equal pay for equal work and to equal opportunities for education and employment. In the church, we have discovered that God calls women to positions of leadership, including the ordained ministry.

As we look at these developments, it is easy to see that the church has been responding to challenges and examples set by society at large. This has led some to say that the resulting changes are uncalled for—after all, the church should lead, not follow! Yet, if we look at the case of Cornelius and what God did through this Roman centurion in the mostly pagan city of Caesarea, we see that God does sometimes call the church to new obedience. God sometimes moves the church into the future by calls that come not from the center of the church itself from its long-established members and leaders but from recent converts and people who have come to faith by routes different than ours.

A Closing Act of Witness and Worship ■

Invite the group to mention people through whom they have learned something important for their Christian lives, even though such people may not be leaders, pastors, or teachers in the church. As group members speak, make a list. End the session with a prayer of thanksgiving for all these people mentioned.

Session Eight

Jesus Calls Into Mission

Session Focus ■

This chapter focuses on the Great Commission both as a calling and as a sending. Before we can be sent, we must be called. Thus, this entire series of studies we now complete, while focusing on calling, has the purpose of sending us out in witness and service.

Session Objective ■

To help us see that we have all come to faith through the witness of others, and that we are therefore a link in a long chain that must not be interrupted and to show us the all-encompassing scope of the power and the call of Jesus.

Session Preparation ■

Think about how you came to faith. Make a list of the people who brought you to faith. As far as you can, list some of those who in turn brought them to faith. Go as far back as you can.

Choose from among these activities and discussion starters to plan your lesson.

(Matthew 28:16-20)

Where Are We in the Story?

Matthew 28:16-20 is so well known that sometimes we think there is no need to read or study it again. It tells us that we are to go and make disciples—tell them the good news of the gospel, bring them to church, baptize them, teach them. Yet even such a well-known passage can gain new meaning with each new reading.

In this case, I would like to invite you to read the passage placing you in a different place in what you read. Allow me to explain this statement. Whenever we see a play, read a novel, or watch a movie, we tend to place ourselves in the story. Actually, this is what makes some classical works of literature so powerful. *Hamlet* is great, not just because of its words and its cadences but also because as we watch it we see Hamlet and others asking questions that—perhaps not as clearly or as dramatically—we too have asked. When I first read *Don Quixote*, I laughed because I found many of his dreams and misunderstandings disarmingly reminiscent of many of my own dreams and misunderstandings. At that point Sancho Panza, his fat and earthy squire, appeared to me too realistic and uninspiring—perhaps reminding me of the many times my parents and others had to

Where Are We in the Story? ■

What are your favorite movies, novels, or plays? Is there a particular character in them with whom you identify?

Read aloud Matthew 28:16-20 to the entire group. Now take two or three aside and read the passage to them within the hearing of the others. When you come to the words "of all nations," point to the rest of the group. How did the reading seem different?

clip my wings of fancy. Much later I read the same book. This time, however, I tried to understand Sancho Panza and to identify with him. Now the book was not so much about an exceptional dreamer following his own delusive imagination as it was about this common man, so much like me, who followed while doubting, who dreamed while calculating. Thus, the meaning of the book was enriched as I identified with a different character. (Perhaps some day I shall try reading it again, now identifying with Rocinante, Don Quixote's nag whose name means "used to be a charger"!)

Biblical passages also are enriched as we practice reading them while identifying with different characters or situations. The parable of the prodigal means one thing if we identify, as we usually do, with the son who goes to a distant land, and quite another if we identify with the other son who resents his brother's homecoming celebration, and still another if we read it while identifying with the loving and forgiving father. The Book of Revelation is a book of terror if we identify with the order it declares to be passing, or a book of joy if, like its first readers, we are excluded, oppressed, and even persecuted by that order.

Looking again at the text we are studying today, usually called "the Great Commission," it is possible to read it, as we usually do, as those commissioned by Jesus to proclaim the gospel. We shall return to this thought later in our study. Now, however, I suggest we look at the text from the other side: not as those who are being sent, but as those to whom the apostles were sent.

Historically, there is much to commend this other—if perhaps uncommon—reading. The words in the Great Commission that our English Bibles translate as "the nations" *(ta ethne)* were used among Jews at the time to refer to the Gentiles. Most of us who read and study these words today are Gentiles by birth, rather than Jews. If the commission was to go to "the nations," we were those nations. We were the ones to whom the promises made to Abraham had not been made. We were the ones outside the covenant. We were not so much the carriers of the mission as we were its recipients.

A Long and Twisting Chain

A Long and Twisting Chain

Think about some of your ancestors in the faith. List some of the admirable ones—martyrs, saintly monks and nuns, devoted missionaries, exemplary pastors, and so forth. Think also of some who may not have been so admirable and yet are also part of our religious ancestry— crusaders, conquistadores, colonial exploiters, slave traders and owners, and so forth. Reflect on the winding ways by which the faith has come to you.
What does this "long and twisting chain" say to you about the call of God through Jesus Christ?

We are Christians today because Jesus has called us. He has called us through others— through others who themselves were called, and who upon being called also received the commission to go and teach. Therefore, while not forgetting that we have been commissioned to go and teach, it is also important to remember that we have been called and taught by others. With regard to the Great Commission, we stand at both ends. Not only are we sent, before being sent we have had others sent to us.

At the conclusion of this study on Jesus who calls, let us pause to consider how we have been called. Between the time when Jesus gave his followers the Great Commission and the present stand generations who, as so many links in a chain, were taught so they could teach, were the recipients of the gospel so they could proclaim it and pass it on. We are Christians today because we are part of that great and uninterrupted chain of teachers and learners, of learners who became teachers, of disciples who became apostles.

A Chain Both Long and Short

A Chain Both Long and Short

Go back as far as you can along the chain of people

That chain is both longer and shorter than we think. It is longer in the sense that it that brought the gospel to you. Write, for instance, "my parents, their pastor," and so on. If some of your "links" are still accessible to you, ask them about their ancestors in the faith. Think about the differences in their personalities and their lives. What did you learn from them? What in their witnesses was similar? different?

includes a wide variety of people. Among our ancestors in the faith probably stand people whom we remember and whose memory we cherish—our parents, a Sunday school teacher, an adult who befriended us in our youth, someone who brought us to church. But there also stand many whom we have never met, and who would find us and our lives strange, for they lived long ago, and in very different circumstances. There are probably long-forgotten missionaries who risked their lives so that some of our ancestors might believe; monks who copied the Bible, and thus transmitted and preserved it for future generations; common folk who simply taught their faith to their children; scholars who studied ancient languages and translated the Bibles that we now take for granted. There may even be some people whom we would not admire today. There may be warriors who "converted" other nations through the "persuasion" of the sword. There is also the possibility that among your ancestors in the faith there may be a slave owner who exploited and abused others of your ancestors in the faith, but from whom somehow, strange as it may seem, your physical ancestors learned of Jesus and the Bible message. The line that joins us to those who first heard the Great Commission is long and strange indeed!

But the line is also shorter than we think. If someone was 15 years old when she first heard the gospel from one of the original disciples, and told the story to another 15-year-old some 40 years later at 55, and that second person repeated the story when he or she in turn was 55, and so on, it would take only 50 people to link us all the way back to the apostles! Think about it. Fifty people!

Fewer than those who ride with you in a crowded bus or in an almost empty jetliner!

Look at the Great Commission again, and consider the long and winding chain through which the message has come to you. The sheer variety of people who form the links in the chain alerts us to the first basic point that we must not forget as we complete this series of studies: Jesus calls many different people, in incredibly varied circumstances, in myriad ways, to do thousands of different things. We are now completing our study of how and to what Jesus calls us. As you review that study, never forget this long and twisting line of witnesses—heroic witnesses, reluctant witnesses, daring witnesses, obedient witnesses, sinful witnesses, confused witnesses; but all witnesses whom Jesus called and employed. Do not forget that you are heir to that long and twisting line, and that so is every other believer around you—some whose calling may seem strange to you, but who nevertheless may well be part of this long chain of witnesses that God has raised and continues raising through the ages.

The second point that we should remember is that each person in the link of that long chain of people in turn had someone to teach him or her. The disciples were called by Jesus and turned into apostles—as when the fisherman Simon became the apostle Peter. The first generation after the apostles—people such as Stephen, Lydia, and Priscilla—had to learn from the apostles or from other believers. None was born already knowing or already believing. Even Paul, before his experience on the road to Damascus, had been taught by the Old Testament; and after that experience, Paul was taught by Ananias and many others. All the apostles were disciples before they became teachers. It was their learning from others that made it possible for them to teach others. Had they not learned, they would never have been able to teach. Had they not taught, the chain would have been interrupted. Because they both learned and taught, we are here!

Third, this reminds us that we all need to be taught by others, and that much of what we do in our teaching is to adapt and transmit what we ourselves were taught. If we can teach others how to read, it is because we were taught how to read. We may develop new methods of teaching, but we will still be teaching essentially what we learned from others. Furthermore, even those supposedly new methods will most likely be variations and combinations of various things we have learned from others. The same is true of the faith. This is why the call to the family of faith that we studied in Session Five is so important. In calling us into this community, the Lord has made us part of that long chain of teachers and witnesses. We all must have been taught by others. Our own experiences, and the varying conditions in which the church finds itself, may lead to new teachings, new practices, and so forth. But still, no one can simply start a new chain, so to speak, from scratch, as if never taught by anyone else, or as if having no link with that long chain of learners and teachers. There have been cases of people who have found a Bible or a New Testament and been converted without anyone telling them personally about the faith. But even such people have been taught by others. They have been taught by those who wrote Scripture, by those who preserved it, by those who translated it, even by whoever left a Bible or a New Testament where they could find it.

Thus, even such converts have been taught by others. They too are part of that long, winding, uninterrupted chain linking every believer to the first believers.

If we then look at how short the entire chain from the apostles to us may be (no more than 50 people), this reminds us of the importance of every witness and every generation. If at any point in that chain a single link had failed, the chain would have been interrupted; and we would not be here. If the apostles had simply gone home, we would not be here. If some monk had not labored long hours at copying the Bible, we would not have a Bible. If others had not toiled at translating it into English, most of us would not be able to read it. If some had not printed it, most of us would not be able to afford a Bible. And what is true of the Bible is also true of Christian teachings and practices. In that long chain of transmission—of learning and teaching—every link is essential.

We Too Are Part of the Chain

We Too Are Part of the Chain

What insights do you gain about your role as a link in the chain as you consider the chain through which the faith has come to you? Who are the persons in your life that may be links for the next generation? In what ways, in words or in actions, can you be a stronger link in the chain?

For us today, this means that we must not see ourselves as the end of the chain but rather as what will most likely become another necessary link for future generations. We learn because others can teach us. But we also learn because we are called to teach. We listen as past generations speak; but we do not listen only for ourselves, for we are responsible for taking up the role of speakers for future generations.

The study you now complete is part of this long chain. Just about everything I have written here I have learned from others who preceded me in the chain. I can write these things because I have been taught by various members of that chain—by my parents and

A "Genealogical Tree" of Faith ■

As a group, prepare a schematic "genealogical tree" of your faith. However, instead of placing yourself at the bottom, place each of the members as a leaf, and go back to the twigs that they have in common; then go to the branches, until you get to the trunk, which will be the first disciples. (Naturally, you will have to use your imagination to fill the gaps. But you should be able to find out the founders of your church, of your denomination, and so on.)

my church in Cuba many years ago; by scholars at the seminary in Cuba and at Yale University; by an illiterate old man in a poverty-stricken barrio; by books I have read, some of them written centuries ago; by colleagues at various times. In short, I can write these things because quite a few people before me, some of them consciously and others even unwittingly, took upon themselves the Great Commission. And in a very real sense I am still the recipient of that chain. I still read a sermon by John Wesley, or a prayer of John Calvin; and through the written works, they teach me. Every time I go to church; every time I read or hear Scripture; every time I learn anything, both with my head and with my heart, I am the beneficiary of that long chain linking me to the first disciples.

You too are part of that chain. As you read this book and studied the passages to which it refers, you were mostly at the learning end of that chain. That is good. The learning end is the growing end. Hopefully, as you read these chapters, you were taught, not just by me, but also by that long chain of witnesses and teachers from whom I have learned. But your very process of learning, of digging deeper into your faith and the faith of the church, also means that you are one more link in the chain. You are being called, not only to learn but also to share whatever you learn. You are being called, not only to meet Jesus at a deeper level but also to speak of Jesus to others. You and I, part of "the nations" to whom Jesus sent his first disciples, are also the disciples being sent to the nations.

An All-Encompassing Gospel ■

Look at the three places in the text where the words

An All-Encompassing Gospel

Now let's look again at the text. Most often when studying this text we focus our *all* and *always* appear. Mark them. Ask two sets of questions: (1) Are there any "nations"—places, countries, people—to whom you believe the disciples of Jesus should not go, because there is no hope for them? In what sense would you say that Jesus has been given "all authority" over them? How can you "go" to them? (Think of "nations" not only in the sense of countries but also in the sense of "Gentiles," people who reject the gospel. It could just be a friend or an acquaintance whom refuses to believe.) (2) Jesus says "always." Are there times or places where you feel forsaken, as if Jesus were no longer with you? Share these experiences. Consider as a group what you can do for each other when the promise, "I am with you always," seems hard to believe.

attention on *what* the disciples are to do: They are to go, make disciples, baptize, and teach. But in so doing we may miss the why they are to do all these things. Verses 19 and 20, which are the ones most often quoted, begin with the words, "Go therefore." One never begins a speech or a point with "therefore." On the contrary, the very word *therefore* implies that there is a reason previously given for what follows. I say, for instance, "It is raining, therefore the ball game has been cancelled." What goes before the *therefore* tells people the reason for what comes after. Thus, we must not read the Great Commission as beginning with verse 19 but rather with verse 18, before the *therefore*.

When thus read, the reason for the Great Commission is clear, and perhaps surprising: "All authority in heaven and on earth has been given to me. Go therefore. . . ." The apostles are to go—we are to go, not because Jesus wants to be Lord of all, but rather because in a way he is already Lord of all! Notice the repetition of the word *all*: "All authority. . . . All nations. . . ." Jesus is not sending the disciples into an absolutely alien world but into a world over which he already has authority. (Remember our very first study, when we considered what John says about the Word that was incarnate in Jesus being the same Word through whom all things were made.)

Think about that. When Jesus sends his disciples to "the nations," to *ta ethne*, to us who were Gentiles, he is already Lord of *all* the nations, Lord of heaven and earth. We simply did not know it. Jesus is sending his disciples into a Roman Empire that will persecute them and kill several of them. But in a way Jesus is already Lord of the Roman Empire. It just doesn't know it, and therefore rebels! Today, Jesus is sending us into a world that lives by other values, that pays little attention to his teachings, that perhaps even thinks that those teachings are no longer relevant. But of that world too, Jesus is Lord. It just doesn't know it, and therefore it rebels! Can you believe it? Peter and James knew something about the Roman Empire that the emperor and the Roman Senate did not even imagine. Had the emperor and the Senate been told, they probably would have laughed. But they would have been wrong, and Peter and James were right! We too know something about the world that the world does not know about itself: It belongs to Jesus Christ!

Today, we are being called by the same Jesus of the Great Commission. We are being made part of that long chain of witnesses. We are being sent into a society that seems to have less and less use for the Christian faith, where egotistical values of self-promotion, of accumulation of wealth, and of personal interests seem to prevail. But we know something about that society that it does not know about itself: All authority in heaven and on earth—and in this society, and in any other society—has been given to Jesus.

Look at it another way. When Jesus told his disciples to "go therefore," he was telling them that they should go because he would already be there. That is why the Great Commission—and the Gospel of Matthew—ends with the promise, "Remember, I am with you always, to the end of the age." Since all authority in heaven and in earth has been given to him, there is no place we can go where he is not Lord. His lordship may be ignored, resisted, or even denied. But it cannot be undone. He is already there before we get there—wherever "there" may be. The commission is universal (*all* the nations) because the authority and the presence of Jesus are all-encompassing, both in time and in space ("*all* authority in heaven and on earth"; "*always,* to the end of the age").

Jesus Calls in Order to Send

Jesus Calls in Order to Send ■

If you are tempted to think that your witness is not important, think about where the world would be if those 11 disciples had decided that their witness was not important. Try to imagine where you would be. We are all the beneficiaries of an inheritance that has come to us through witnessing. Complete the sentence: As a link in the great chain of witnesses, I am passing on the message by _____.

Throughout this study, we have considered the call of Jesus. The first session sought to place this within the context of Creation, pointing out the cosmic dimensions of the power of Jesus to call. After that, we dealt with specific cases of people whom Jesus called, in other words, with the callings of his disciples, for after all a disciple of Jesus is simply one who heeds his call. It is fitting for the passage we are now studying to be our last, for not only does it come at the end of the Gospel of Matthew, it actually deals with the "end," that is, with the purpose of the call. As we have seen, the call of Jesus has many dimensions. It is a call to joy, to suffering, to death, to life eternal. Ultimately, however, it is a call to go. At the end of the Gospel, when Jesus is about to leave those whom he called several years before, he tells them to go: "Go therefore to all the nations." He calls them not just to make them his followers but also so they can call others to follow as well. He calls his disciples in order to make them apostles. He calls in order to send.

It is important for us to keep this in mind as we conclude and review this study. As we study and heed the call of Jesus, we are blessed. We are edified, both as individuals and as a group. But we must always remember that our calling is not an end in itself. The purpose of our calling is not just so that each one of us might be more blessed, or

Close With Worship ■

As a way to conclude and review what you have studied, end with a prayer in which you take in order the titles of each session. Thus one person says: "We thank you, Lord, that you call us into existence." Allow a moment of silence. Then another person says: "We thank you, Lord, that you call us into discipleship." After some silence, another says: "We thank you, Lord, that you call us by naming and renaming us." And so on. End with a prayer of thanksgiving for all the people—most of them unknown to us—who are part of our "family tree" of faith, that long line through which the gospel has come to us.

more saintly, or more joyous, or better informed. The purpose of our calling is also that each one of us may understand that our call impels us to call others.

If we followed these study sessions as a group, the purpose of our sessions was not just that our group might be edified, or that we might relate better among ourselves. The purpose was to call the entire group to open itself up as a group that not only has a calling but also is calling others into discipleship— and is inviting them to call others, thus continuing a chain of called callers that has persisted for 20 centuries—and will continue "to the end of the age."

If this sounds difficult, if the forces of opposition seem too strong, if it seems that there are places or times where we cannot follow our call by calling others, remember that the Word who in the beginning called all things into existence, the Word incarnate in Jesus, sends us to *all* the nations, that he is with us *always*, and that *all* authority belongs to him!